How to write
effective reports

How to write effective reports

Second edition

John E Sussams

Gower

Published by
Gower Publishing Company Limited
Gower House
Croft Road
Aldershot
Hants GU11 3HR
England

Gower Publishing Company
Old Post Road
Brookfield
Vermont 05036
USA

British Library Cataloguing in Publication Data
Sussams, John E. (John Edward)
  How to write effective reports.–2nd. ed.
  1. Reports. Composition
  I. Title
  808.066

ISBN 0 566 02911 1

Printed in Great Britain by
Billing & Sons Ltd, Worcester

Contents

List of illustrations   vii

Preface to the second edition   ix

1   Why a report?   1
Working papers · Other means of communication

2   Structure   15
The summary · The main body of the report ·
Complex ideas · Appendices · Charts and diagrams ·
Presentation of statistical data

3   Layout   37
Margins · Paragraphs · Headings ·
Numbering of diagrams, tables, and appendices ·
Spacing · When to print on both sides of the paper ·
Summary

4   Language   51

5   Spelling and punctuation   69
Spelling · Punctuation · Italics · Numbers
Abbreviations

6   Materials and equipment   83
Covers · Binding · Paper · Typefaces ·
Reprographic methods · Charts and diagrams

Contents

7 **Planning** 101
The schedule · The skeleton report · Assembling the
raw material · Drafting · Timing · Editorial control

Exercises 111
Comment · Examples · Self-analysis

Suggested further reading 127

Illustrations

1.1 Stages in report preparation · 3

2.1 Title page layout · 17

2.2 Contents page · 18

2.3 Graph showing economic batch quantity · 29

2.4 Graph showing number of horses and tractors used for agricultural purposes in Great Britain · 33

2.5 Pie chart showing consumers' expenditure · 34

2.6 Bar chart showing depreciation and maintenance costs over ten years for a 32-ton gross articulated vehicle · 35

2.7 Frequency polygon showing distribution of mark-ups in the retailing of domestic electrical appliances · 36

3.1 Guide sheet for report typist · 40

3.2 Example of report page layout · 49

6.1 Types of binding · 89

6.2 Type styles · 92

6.3 Proportional spacing · 95

Preface to the second edition

This book is based on many years' experience of report writing and of helping other people to write their reports. In the course of this experience I have learned that there are three areas in particular where the novice report writer needs assistance. These are: (1) the constructing of sentences and paragraphs, (2) the structuring of the report and (3) the planning of the investigation or project to include sufficient time for report writing.

I have had many long and learned discussions concerning the merits and demerits of particular rules and conventions and I have tried, throughout the book, wherever one of these rules or conventions is discussed, to give sound, practical reasons for following it or not following it, as the case may be. If you know why you should do something (use active verbs, keep paragraphs short, not split infinitives, etc.) then you are more likely to do it.

Another important lesson, which my work for large industrial organisations and government departments has taught me, is that the quality of the report reflects the quality of the work about which the report is written. You cannot do a bad job and then write a good report about it. Deficiencies in the one will show up as deficiencies in the other – even if the English is impeccable. You can do a good job and skimp the report. However, if you do this and the report is the only permanent record of the work, nobody will know or remember how well the job was done. On the other hand, the discipline of writing a good report, of proceeding from the facts through careful analysis to the logical conclusions, is almost a guarantee that the work will be done thoroughly and methodically.

For this new edition of the book I have added a section on 'Complex Ideas' in Chapter 2. This is because the essential content of a report, while necessarily expressed within a framework of chapters, sections, paragraphs and sentences, with appropriate diagrams and illustrations, is information. The report is a channel for information but the information itself also needs to be organised in a manner which facilitates communication. Thus the way in which complex ideas are developed and the language in which they are expressed are equally important.

I have also revised and updated the section on 'Word Processors' in Chapter 6 to reflect the latest developments in this important field. Indeed, since the introduction of the latest word processing and graphics packages, the traditional typewritten report with its hand-drawn diagrams may no longer be acceptable.

In this book I consider not only the content of a report, but also its physical appearance. The former may be likened to a product, the latter to its packaging. The production of a report should be considered as a project in itself or, rather, as a project within the project which is the subject of the report. The author or editor of a report is the link between the research or fieldwork performed by the operational staff and the administrative machine which is geared to the production and distribution of the required number of copies of the report, on time and error free. It is just as important that typing, duplicating and other office services should be well organised and efficient as that the report itself should be well written in the first place.

Finally, I have provided some exercises designed to cover the linguistic points made in the chapters. Practice makes perfect.

John E Sussams
London

1

Why a report?

A report serves two purposes. First, it provides a permanent, comprehensive and coherent account of an investigation, study or piece of research. Second, it provides information which is required for decision taking. Those are the obvious reasons for writing a report. But there are also two less obvious reasons which may be seen, ultimately, to be more important, at least to the report writer. The first is that the form and quality of the report is an indication, indeed, as will be shown, a determinant, of the quality of the work discussed in the report. The second is that the author of the report will be judged, to some extent, on the quality of his written work. Promotion may actually depend on it. To put this another way: unless you do the work thoroughly you will not be able to write a satisfactory report and if you do not write a satisfactory report you may well be deemed to be incompetent. It follows that, in perfecting the art of report writing, you will at the same time be improving your performance as a manager, project leader, researcher or investigator as the case may be. For the report is an essential part of the work. It is not simply a chore at the end of an investigation. On the contrary, the production of a report may in some cases be the main purpose of the work.

The very fact that the report will describe, clearly and in logical sequence, the steps which have been taken to complete the work, helps to ensure that those steps are actually taken. How often does a disorganised project leader find that, during the last week of an exercise, when he is frantically writing his report, there is some vital piece of information which is missing? What does he do? He either delays the report while he gets the missing data or he attempts to cover up his omission by writing something vague in the report. What should he have done? He should have planned the report at an early stage in the exercise. Then he would have had a list of all the items to be included in the report and he would have arranged to collect the information as and when required. The report is a kind of model of the whole exercise and the preparation of the report is a mini-project within a project. This is true whether the subject of the report is a scientific experiment, a business proposition or a major survey for a government department.

The purpose of this first chapter is to discuss certain aspects of the work itself since, to the extent that a report is not based on 'desk research' alone, the work has to be organised in such a way that it produces the information which the client actually wants to see embodied in the report which is finally submitted to him. The problem may be described with reference to a simple diagram – Figure 1.1.

Working papers

A report is a definitive document, the end product of an exercise. It presents information in a very special way. However, nearly all the information contained in a report has already been written down and collected in what are

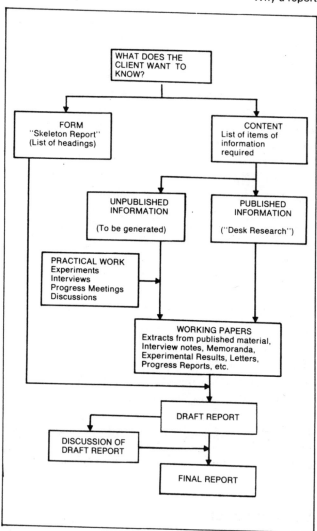

Figure 1.1
Stages in report preparation. Although practical work may occupy more than three-quarters of the time, this work must be planned to fit into the overall framework of the project and geared to the production of relevant information.

generally described as the 'working papers'. It is not unusual for the volume of working papers to be ten or even twenty times the volume of the report itself. It is therefore axiomatic that if the working papers are comprehensive and well organised the writing of the report itself will be that much more simple. Indeed, passages can be lifted verbatim from well written notes. Working papers may be categorised as:

(a) Background information: relevant documents already published – reports, press cuttings, articles from the trade and technical press, learned journals, etc. and correspondence related to the setting up of the exercise. All these documents need to be perused before any practical work is undertaken and before any further documents are written. It would be unwise to start work without knowing what has already been done in the area: one would be in danger of, as they say, re-inventing the wheel. In the final report reference is normally made to this background information either by appending a 'list of documents consulted' or by providing a brief summary at an early point in the report, before coming on to the part which deals with analysis and comment.

(b) Planning information: the lists of subjects which need to be covered in the report, the people who need to be approached, the plan of work for the whole investigation (who is going to do what and when), related notes and correspondence.

(c) Documents required to generate data: letters asking people specific questions or setting up meetings to discuss specific topics, aide-memoires (for example, as used by interviewers to remind them of the questions they will be asking) and formal questionnaires. All these documents need to be worded with great care and tact. Do not ask for information unless you are quite sure it is necessary. Ask for both qualitative and quantitative information so that if the latter is not available at least some inferences can be made from the former.

(d) Data: the facts and figures, charts and diagrams, results of experiments, completed questionnaires, etc., which will have to be analysed in order to reach conclusions. If any of this information is required as 'evidence' in the report it is prudent to write it up neatly at the time it is produced so that it can be included, with the minimum of alteration, as an appendix or supplement to the report. If this task of 'writing up' is left to the end it is certain that memories will have faded, it may not be possible to decipher some of the rough notes and there will be errors and omissions. There is also a danger that the typing service will become overloaded at a critical time and checking will be more difficult.

(e) Progress reports: In any major investigation it is necessary to keep track of progress, to take note of what individual members of the team have been doing, whom they have seen, what they have found out, any difficulties they have encountered, any particular items of information which could significantly affect the work of others. These reports are generally discussed either at regular intervals throughout the exercise (the monthly progress meeting) or at the logical break points at the end of each phase of the work. These meetings serve not only to help co-ordinate and control the work but also to keep the client *au fait*, so that he can make useful comments and so that he has early warning of any surprising conclusions which may have been reached and which may lead him to wish to change the direction in which the exercise is going or to expand the terms of reference. The progress report is a means of sorting the wheat from the chaff as you go along. The final report is a rearrangement of the information which has already been sifted and a drawing of conclusions.

Other means of communication

The report is just one of several means of communication. All have their place and most of them will in fact be utilised at some point during the course of the investigation of which the report itself is the culmination. It is therefore worth paying some attention to these other means of communication since for the report itself to be successful the whole exercise must be successful. Every letter, depending on how it is phrased, every telephone call, depending on how it is conducted, can either speed up or delay the work.

The report is not written directly from experience but indirectly from other written material. The preparation of this other material, even if it is mostly rejected or rewritten, is nevertheless part of the report writing process. Moreover, the basic disciplines which apply to writing reports apply to most other forms of written communication. Possible exceptions include poetry, legal documents and the shorthand or cryptic notes that one writes for oneself and which have to be re-written anyway if the thoughts they contain are ever to be communicated to a third party or even recalled at a later date by the note taker.

The documents from which the author of a report will be working and which constitute the interface between the work itself and the report – the definitive account of that work — consist partly of documents which already exist (and from which extracts may be taken or summaries made) and partly of documents which the author or other members of the investigating team have caused to be generated. In the latter case the form and the content of the document which you ultimately use is to a large extent determined by the form of your own request for information. So how do you ask for information?

The telephone call

There is little doubt that the most effective way of obtaining information which is not available from the library is the face to face interview. The quickest way to set up a meeting is to telephone the person concerned and find out when he will be free. That first telephone call is therefore critical. Even if the person concerned is part of your organisation and even if you have every right to expect his co-operation, he can, if he so chooses, be most unhelpful. He may say he is too busy to see you; he may ask you to write, setting out exactly what you want and why; he may refer you to someone else who in his turn finds that he is not the right person to deal with your enquiry; you may get no further than a secretary or an assistant. You must persist.

The best plan is to write down the points you would include in a letter and then ensure that you communicate these points, clearly and distinctly over the telephone. With luck it will not be necessary to elaborate on these points and the meeting will be set up as required. If a long conversation ensues then at least you will know that you have captured the person's interest and you may have got some of the information you want in that first call. Unless you have managed to set up your meeting for the same day the efficient thing to do is to confirm your appointment in writing and at the same time re-iterate the points on which you are seeking guidance. Your intitial telephone call should cover the following points:

- Say who you are and whom you represent.
- Say who has asked you to do what.
- Say that there is certain information about whatever the subject is, that you understand the person you are telephoning may be able to help you to obtain.
- Ask whether he will be free within the next few days to spare you half an hour or so of his time so that you can discuss the details.

Be prepared to answer two likely questions:

- What is the purpose of the investigation?
- What information is it, exactly, that you want?

It is necessary to think out a short and convincing answer to the first question as opposed to a long rambling explanation. As regards the second question, do not ask for whatever is available and do not be so precise that the probable response will be 'Sorry, but we do not have that information'. Say that, for example, you want details of production by volume and value going back a few years. Then wait for the face to face meeting to find out whether the available figures are weekly or monthly, whether there is a breakdown by product group or by customer type or both.

It is quite likely that there is more information available then you actually need and you must resist the temptation to plough through masses of irrelevant data. It is equally likely that some of the data you need is missing and you will have to decide whether to set up a special exercise to obtain it or whether some estimate can be provided.

The interview

Once you are face to face with the person concerned you will find that there are a variety of questions you can ask which you would have found it difficult to ask on the telephone or to put down on paper. Some of these may be key questions, others interesting but not vital. Provide yourself with an interview guide so that you get the most you can out of what may be a fairly short session. Make sure you list all the important subjects you wish to cover and also any general questions which you can use to open up a subject or develop a conversation when the opportunity arises. Examples of such general questions are:

- Are there any problems with suppliers?
- What were the underlying causes of that recent labour dispute?
- Has there been any improvement since the recent re-organisation?

Quite often, as a result of asking general questions of the above type, a very interesting conversation develops and subjects are discussed which throw a new light on the problem but which it would never have occurred to you to ask in a formal questionnaire.

The questionnaire

Written questions should be phrased in such a way that simple answers can be given: facts and figures rather than opinions. Remember that when there are numerous alternatives it may be neater (and make the questionnaire look shorter) if you list only the two or three most likely and then write 'Other, please specify,' to cover the rest. It is also a good idea to divide the questionnaire into sections where the first section contains questions relating to the most important information which is likely to be available. The remaining sections would ask for detailed figures which may be more difficult to obtain and may in fact be omitted. If a questionnaire comes back with 'Not available' against numerous items you have asked for there is not much you can do about it within the time available. If a telephone call or a follow-up interview elicits more information then this could be an indication that the basic questions were badly phrased in the first place. Ask for information which *ought* to be available. Then, if it is not, perhaps the client will see the need for it and ask you to advise on the provision of a system so that the required information will be available in the future.

When sending a letter in which you are asking for information, try to ensure that the letter is not more than one page long. If there is a long list of items required, attach this as a separate questionnaire so that the letter itself remains short. This letter should state succinctly what is required and why it is required and should of course be very polite: 'I should be most grateful if . . .' etc.

If you have to conduct a survey as part of your study, this will involve asking the same questions of a large number of respondents. The questions should be carefully worded so as to avoid ambiguity. They should also be designed to facilitate analysis. This means that, wherever possible, the questions should require simple 'yes/no', 'multiple choice', numerical or one-word answers. The sheet should be laid out so that the answers always appear on the right. This makes it easy to count, copy or check the replies to each question.

The presentation

One of the best possible ways of ensuring that the final report is acceptable is to make an oral presentation of the main findings fairly near the end of the exercise. At this point most of the work will have been done but there will still be time to check up on any points which may be raised in the course of a discussion of the findings.

In the case of a major investigation involving the collection of a large amount of data, it is usually a good idea to arrange for an interim presentation, the sole purpose of which is to 'sign off' the data. All the key facts which have been collected should be summarised and presented at this meeting, and an opportunity provided for the client to correct any errors and fill any gaps. Thereafter both you and your client will know that any conclusions which may be drawn will be based on agreed facts and figures.

The oral presentation will gloss over the introductory material, the reasons for the study and so on and it will not go laboriously through all the business of collecting data and analysing it. It will concentrate on the conclusions and hint at the recommendations which are likely to be made in the final report. The presenter will have available arguments and evidence – a few telling examples rather an an enormous catalogue – so that, if there is any query concerning one of conclusions, he can go into greater detail. If evidence is not available then perhaps the conclusion is not justified. The ideal format for an oral presentation is very simple. It is the format for a well prepared lesson – with plenty of visual aids:

- Indicate the structure of the presentation by putting up a list of headings.

- Go through the list, making use of examples, illustrations and diagrams.

- Pull together all the conclusions (from the preceding examples) and present these in the form of a list.

- Ask for questions and comments and lead the discussion of these.

- Ask questions to see if your audience has fully appreciated the implications of your conclusions.

- Round off the discussion with a summary of any new or modified conclusions which need to be incorporated in the final report and draw attention to any additional work which will need to be performed.

- Follow this up with a memorandum within twenty-four hours.

Visual aids

Choose visual aids to suit the occasion. How many people will be attending? Where will the presentation be held? There are three main levels of presentation, depending on whether there will be only two or three people, up to half a dozen people or a larger audience. For the very small group, where you sit in someone's office, round a desk or small table, the best visual aids are:

- The 'presenter' – an arrangement for holding small flip charts which you can turn over as you talk.

- The 'presentation book' – a book of transparent plastic pockets into which charts and diagrams can be slipped and the pages turned as you talk.

The above can be supplemented with handouts (tables of figures and key diagrams). A photocopy of a set of all the charts which have been used to illustrate the talk can be left at the end of the meeting. If the office is equipped with a blackboard or whiteboard this may be useful and, as a last resort, to illustrate a point, there is always pencil and paper. However, to inspire confidence and give a professional appearance to the work, it is always best to prepare charts and diagrams in advance, making sure that the lines are clear and the lettering neat.

For the group of half a dozen people who may be assembled round a boardroom table it is even more important that charts, diagrams and handouts should be prepared in advance. If a 'presenter' is used it should be a large one, designed to take A3 or brief sized sheets and the lettering should be sufficiently large for someone at the other end of a long table to be able to read it. Use thick, coloured felt pens and letters between half an inch and an inch high.

For a larger audience a larger stand will be required, with larger charts and larger lettering. It is a good idea to have some blank sheets and the use of a second stand or board so that points requiring further explanation can be illustrated as and when necessary without disturbing the main sequence of charts.

An alternative to the use of flip charts is the use of the overhead projector or the slide projector. There is not normally time to prepare 35mm slides for what is, after all, only a progress meeting. However, transparencies for an overhead projector take no more skill, time or effort than flip charts. The important point is that the machine should be in working order (make sure there is a spare bulb!) and that the lettering should be clear. Typescript is too small for most audiences, even for those in the front row. There should not normally be more than half a dozen lines of print on the screen. If it is necessary to show large tables of figures or complex diagrams, have copies made and hand them out.

The object of the presentation is twofold. First, it provides the client with a résumé of the work which has been performed so that he has a clear idea of what to expect in the final report. Second, it enables those who have been doing the work to obtain feedback so that any areas where information is lacking or explanations are inadequate can be improved in the final version.

Effective communication, whether by the spoken word or the written word, whether it is a five-minute telephone call or a twenty-five-minute formal presentation, a one-page letter or a fifty-page report, depends on adequate preparation. It is not reasonable to expect the average manager, project leader or consultant to have the combined skills of a top television interviewer and a top newspaper journalist, a professional actor and a professor of English – as well as being an engineer, architect, accountant or whatever. But it is reasonable to expect him to have done his homework, to be articulate, to be confident on his feet and competent on paper. Naturally, the 'homework' required to produce a fifty-page report is substantially more than that required before making a telephone call, but the principle remains the same: think out what you want to say and know how to say it. If in any doubt, try it out on someone else whose comments are likely to be helpful. This book is concerned with the how rather than the what and with the fifty-page report rather than the five-minute telephone call.

2

Structure

This chapter is concerned with the macrostructure of a report, its division into chapters and sections, the ordering of these and the organisation of summaries, illustrations, diagrams and appendices. Later on in the book the micro-structure of paragraphs, their division into sentences, the construction of these sentences out of words and punctuation marks, will be considered.

As a general rule a report should be thought of as consisting of three parts: an introduction and summary (which will explain the purpose of the report, describe the methods used in the investigation which is the subject of the report, and give the main conclusions and recommendations); the main body (consisting of a series of chapters or sections in logical sequence, subject by subject, arranged so as to present first the findings or evidence, then an analysis of the findings and, finally, the conclusions reached); the appendices (including any necessary notes, tabulations, calculations, references, etc., which are germane to the main argument but which are too long or too technical to be given in the main body of the report).

In addition to the three parts mentioned above there will also be, in front of the report, a title page and a contents page. The importance of these two pages is stressed since, if the title is misleading or there is no list of contents, the report may not be read or consulted by all those for whom it is intended.

The title page is the first page inside the front cover. The title itself should give a clear indication of the subject matter in as few words as possible. It should also indicate the nature of the report, whether it is a draft, interim or final report. Information given on the title page should also include the name of the author or organisation responsible for producing the report, the address, the date of issue, any reference number and any caveat concerning confidentiality, copyright, etc. A suggested layout for a title page is shown in Figure 2.1. In this case the title is printed so that it will show through a window in the report cover. The question of report covers is discussed in Chapter 6.

The contents page should list the chapters and sections within chapters, giving page numbers. The structure of the report will be apparent from the contents page. If chapter and section headings are carefully worded, the contents page can provide the reader with a good indication as to the structure and nature of the report. An example of a contents page is given in Figure 2.2.

The summary

The first section or chapter of a report usually contains a summary. (The word 'chapter' is used to indicate a major subdivision of a report: the word 'section' is used to indicate a subdivision of a chapter. However, a short report may not be divided into chapters but contain only a series of quite short sections.) It is necessary to distinguish between the summary in the first chapter of a report, a summary report and a synopsis or abstract of a

```
┌──────────────────────────────────────────────┐
│                                                │
│                                                │
│        ┌──────────────────────────────┐        │
│        │                              │        │
│        │    XYZ ENGINEERING CO LTD    │        │
│        │        SYSTEMS STUDY         │        │
│        │                              │        │
│        └──────────────────────────────┘        │
│                                                │
│                                                │
│                                                │
│                                                │
│                                                │
│                                                │
│                                                │
│                                                │
│                                                │
│                 Prepared by                    │
│                                                │
│      Fred Smith   Management Consultant        │
│      123 High Street    London SE99 9ES        │
│                                                │
│                February 19XX                   │
│                                                │
└──────────────────────────────────────────────┘
```

Figure 2.1
Title page layout

CONTENTS

1. INTRODUCTION   page 2

    --   Terms of Reference
    --   Summary of Conclusions
    --   Recommendations

2. EXISTING PROCEDURES   page 5

    --   Narrative
    --   Flow Chart
    --   List of items of information for processing
    --   Variations in procedure:
          Exports
          Items remaining in stock over a year

3. COMMENTS ON EXISTING PROCEDURES   page 14

    --   Purchasing
    --   Selling
    --   Receipts
    --   Credit Control
    --   Sales Records
    --   Invoices
    --   Checking Sales Records and Invoices
    --   Ledger Posting
    --   Stock Records
    --   Mailing

4. GENERAL COMMENTS   page 21

    --   Organisation
    --   Office Accommodation

5. PROPOSED PROCEDURES   page 24

    --   Narrative
    --   Flow Chart
    --   Comment

6. SCOPE FOR COMPUTERISATION   page 30

    --   Advantages of computerisation
    --   Feasibility Study
    --   Outline proposal for discussion
    --   Estimated costs and timings

Figure 2.2
Contents page

report. The first chapter of a report may be entitled 'Summary' for convenience but ought properly to be headed 'Introduction, Summary of Conclusions and Recommendations'. However, since this is itself no more than a list of subheadings and since 'Introduction' is also rather vague, it is recommended that the chapter heading should remain simple; the subheadings will in any case have been listed already on the contents page.

The first papragraph of the first chapter of the report should cover the authorisation and purpose of the study: who asked whom to do what and why. It is a brief statement of the problem. Following this introductory paragraph there should be four separate sections each with its own subheading:

- Terms of Reference (or Objectives)
- Approach (or Methodology) – i.e. how the work was performed
- Conclusions
- Recommendations

A summary report is sometimes required as a separate document when the full report is a long one running to, say, a hundred pages or more. In these circumstances a shorter version of, say, ten pages could be useful. Many people would be interested only in this shorter version and there would also be a saving in cost. A summary report would have the form of a one-chapter report, each chapter of the full report being condensed down to a section of the summary report. Note that in the full report the conclusions and recommendations are all brought together at the end of the first chapter as well as being restated in the logical places within the main body of the report. In a substantial report this repetition is useful (a) since some people will only read the first chapter and (b) it helps the reader of the full report to fix the most important points (the conclusions) in his mind. In a short report it is suggested that the conclusions should be given in their logical places, i.e. after the individual arguments which lead up to them. However, the recommendations should be listed at the end of all the arguments since it is desirable that they should all be viewed together.

A synopsis or abstract is a one-page document required to be filed separately, perhaps with reference to certain key words. (If the title has been carefully chosen it will almost certainly include one or more of these key words.) An abstract is often given much wider circulation than the report itself. It is in fact a reminder to some people that the report exists and can be obtained if required. Some people who would not want a shelf full of reports are nevertheless pleased to have a slim file containing abstracts relating to a large number of reports. An abstract should aim to encapsulate the essence of a report in a few sentences. The information given should include: a statement of the problem, the methods used to deal with it, the results obtained, conclusions reached and recommendations made. The abstract should also of course give the title of the report, the date of issue, the reference number and/or author's name and the address from which a copy can be obtained.

The main body of the report

The precise way in which the main body of the report should be subdivided will of course depend on the subject matter. An investigation may divide naturally in a way which enables chapters to be written round each subject. For example, in a company appraisal there could be chapters on Production, Marketing, Financial Control,

Organisation Structure, etc. In a report which deals with one specific problem, say, an investigation of the reasons for delays in invoice passing, the structure of the whole might correspond to the structure of a single chapter in a larger or multi-subject report. This structure should take the form of an introductory paragraph or paragraphs followed by sections which present the facts, analyse the facts and draw conclusions from the analysis.

Every chapter should start with an introductory paragraph before the first subheading appears. This is not simply a device to ensure that the main heading is not immediately followed by a subheading; it also prepares the reader for what is to come by outlining the structure of the whole chapter. In addition, the opening sentences of a chapter can provide an opportunity to 'soften up' the reader by telling him a few things he already knows and understands so that he will be more ready to accept any more surprising and perhaps unpalatable facts which are yet to come.

In the case of the invoice passing problem a logical sequence of sections might be:

- Existing system (description of existing system with flow charts);

- Sample data (analysis of a sample of one hundred invoices showing time from receipt of invoice to posting of cheque to supplier);

- Reasons for delay (detailed analysis of reasons for delays in all cases where delays of more than ten days occurred);

- Possible solutions (steps which might be taken to avoid delays);

- Recommendations (recommended new procedures described with sample documents and flow charts).

The above list of sections corresponds almost exactly to the method of dealing with the actual problem. There is one step missing. This is the discussion which should take place before the final recommendations are made and the finishing touches are given to the report. It is always a good idea to go through the investigation step by step with the client (or whoever it was that asked for the report) and to discuss alternative solutions with him. Then, when he reads the report, the logic will be familiar and the recommendations will come as no surprise. They are therefore more likely to be accepted – and implemented.

No hard and fast rules can be laid down as to the length of chapters and/or sections. A section may consist of only one paragraph or it may require a dozen paragraphs plus diagrams and tabulations. A chapter may contain only one section or it may contain up to a dozen sections. It is desirable from the point of view of comprehension and also from an aesthetic point of view that the chapters of a report should be of roughly equal length and that this should be in the region of five or six pages of text or from fifteen hundred to two thousand words. Longer chapters can be divided into sections or they can be shortened by relegating some of the detail to an appendix.

The reason for stipulating this kind of length is that it is about as much as a busy executive can cope with at one sitting, without interruptions. It is better that he should read five pages than that he should not read fifty. Therefore, if the fifty can be broken up into ten groups of five or five groups of ten and if each of these groups is nicely rounded with a beginning, a middle and an end, then there is some chance that the document will eventually be read and understood and even appreciated. It is particularly important that the first chapter (which contains the summary) should not be much longer than half a dozen pages since the reader will be able to go through it in about fifteen minutes before attending a meeting to discuss the document. This will enable him to refresh his memory or indeed (it has been known!) read it for the first time.

It is also important, for the benefit of executives who are in the habit of 'skip-reading' or who have been on a rapid reading course, that headings should be informative and that no key aspect should be dealt with in the text of the report without a heading and a reference in the contents page to draw attention to it.

Complex ideas

One of the most difficult aspects of report writing is the presentation of complex ideas and arguments. The aim should be to present ideas in an ordered sequence so that the reader will follow the line of reasoning without difficulty. In practice there are only two types of reasoning: deductive and inductive. Deductive reasoning is that which infers the particular from the general, as particular effects may be predicted from known causes. Inductive reasoning is that which infers the general from the particular, as a hypothesis may be formulated on the basis of numerous facts or consistent sets of observations.

A complex argument may thus be represented in the form of a hierarchy or 'family tree' of relatively simple ideas, the most general or abstract ideas being at the 'top' of the tree. One may then argue from the top down or from the bottom up. Only relevant ideas should be included and these should be considered in logical groups, for example:

- parts of a whole: assemblies, subassemblies, components;

- causes of an effect in order of importance;

- events in chronological order; or

- locations by geographical region.

If at the end of an exercise certain conclusions have been reached, it will be sensible to go back over the arguments which led to those conclusions and (a) cut out all material which is irrelevant to those conclusions, and (b) reorganise the relevant material so as to make the argument as easy to follow and as convincing as possible.

For example, a certain company was advised to subcontract its primary transport operations. There was a lot of 'evidence' to support this recommendation. There were also counter arguments. The basic facts were that, compared with the quotations received from third party operators, this company's own costs were exceptionally high, and there appeared to be no way in which they could be reduced to a competitive level. Thus the argument was not about the actual costs but about why they could not be significantly reduced. For, indeed, some of the costs could be reduced. Depreciation and maintenance costs could be reduced by a change of policy. Administrative overheads could be reduced with the introduction of computerised vehicle records. However, the main reason for the inefficiency of the vehicle fleet was the fact that the average distance covered daily with a full load was less than two-thirds of that achieved quite regularly by outside hauliers.

This performance could theoretically be improved by better scheduling, but not without a difficult renegotiation of union agreements. The risk of a damaging industrial dispute was high and in the meantime the company's profits were draining away in excess transport costs. The solution proposed was to subcontract the work to third parties who were prepared not only to purchase the vehicles but also to offer employment to the drivers – under new terms and conditions. The main argument could therefore be presented as follows:

- The cost of primary transport per tonne-mile in this company is 1.5 times the norm for the industry.

- The principal reason, accounting for 80% of the excess cost, is underutilisation of the vehicles' time. (Drivers average only 4 hours a day at the wheel while other hauliers achieve double this amount.)

- A better utilization could be achieved with more flexible shift arrangements requiring more drivers and/ or more overtime. (Vehicles should be on the road up to sixteen hours in twenty-four, with drivers working two shifts.)

- Either (1) the current arrangements, with drivers' hours and conditions tied to those of production workers, would have to be renegotiated; or (2) the company would have to pull out of the transport area and leave it to the 'professionals'.

- Of the two options, the second would appear to be more simple and less risky to implement. Transport costs would be reduced by a third and would be more effectively monitored and controlled.

- Therefore, the recommendation is that the management of the primary transport operation should be subcontracted to third party hauliers. Also, to minimise industrial relations problems, jobs would be offered to drivers who would otherwise be made redundant.

Appendices

There are several kinds of information which should not form part of the main body of a report but which should be relegated to appendices. In general, long and complicated tables of figures, mathematical proofs, long extracts from other reports, sample documents, glossaries, bibliographies, lists of notes and references, should be excluded from the text but included at the back of a report for the benefit of those readers who need to check the detail. An exception to this rule would be where the provision of a particular table of figures is one of the primary objectives of the report.

There should be a reference in the text to any appended material. Sometimes this reference may take the form of an abridged table or a brief summary or highlights from the material which is given more fully in the appendices. If possible tables and diagrams appearing within the main body of the report should occupy less than a page so that any description or discussion can appear on the same page. If this is not possible then the next best thing is to use the opposite page for this purpose (which means that certain sheets will need to be printed on both sides in order to avoid there being openings of two blank pages).

If there are large numbers of notes and references in a report the impression may be given that the author has spent most of his time in a library reading about other people's work rather than getting on with his own practical work. Nevertheless, when other authorities are quoted, it is necessary to indicate the source. This particularly applies to tables of figures and statistics. It may be sufficient to give a full reference on the first occasion and abbreviated references on subsequent occasions (e.g. the author's name only) when it is clear that the same source is being quoted. When there are a number of references it is best to refer to them briefly in the text and to give the full information in a list at the end of the chapter or at the end of the report. For example, 'Smith (1) and Brown (2)'. Footnotes should be avoided because they are distracting and because they make difficulties for the typist. An indication of the convention used can be given on the contents page.

A word of warning on appendices: some authors seem to think that the value of their report will be measured in terms of the number of pages produced and that the easiest way to add weight, both literally and figuratively, to their work is to append twenty or thirty pages of computer output or a great volume of 'raw data'. Occasionally this kind of 'evidence' is required but usually it would be included in the 'working papers', available for inspection if the need arises but not included in the report itself. A report should be as short as possible while adequately covering the subject matter. This may require five pages or it may require fifty. But nobody wants to plough through fifty pages (or even carry them around in a brief case) if there are only five pages of significant information and the rest is just padding.

Charts and diagrams

It is said, not without good cause, that one picture is worth a thousand words. And, one might add, it is worth even more if it is coloured. The fact is that some people are able to grasp the essential nature of a system or of a mathematical relationship or of a statistical pattern from a flow diagram, a graph or a chart, more easily and more immediately than from an elaborate verbal explanation. A reader who lacks the necessary technical background will often be able to interpret a graph correctly even though the mathematical equations represented by the graph may be utterly incomprehensible to him.

Every diagram should be accompanied by a brief explanation and a reference in the text: 'It can be seen from the diagram (Figure 2.1) that . . .' Diagrams should be neat, the lettering on them should be clear and the margins adequate. Choose a scale which enables these criteria to be met. Note that in many areas there are special conventions concerning the way in which flow charts and other diagrams should be drawn. There are special symbols used, for example, in Work Study, in Organisation and Methods, in Systems Analysis, and so on. Remember that the people reading the report may not be familiar with the conventions used and that, if this is so, a key should be given.

There are many different types of diagram, some of the more important of which are worth mentioning here. For the presentation of mathematical relationships there are various kinds of graph. A good example is Figure 2.3 which shows the relationship between batch size (i.e. the quantity of goods manufactured or processed in one batch) and total cost.

Total cost consists of (a) manufacturing costs (itself having fixed and variable components, namely, set-up cost per batch plus variable production cost per unit) and (b) stockholding cost (which is a rate of interest applied to the average value of stock held). It can be seen from the graph:

- That manufacturing cost per unit decreases as batch size increases and that the rate of decrease is very steep at first, becoming less and less steep as batch size increases.

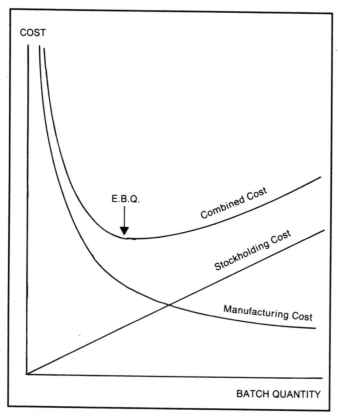

Figure 2.3
Graph showing economic batch quantity (EBQ) (which corresponds with the minimum point on the combined cost curve)

- That stockholding cost increases with batch size and that the rate of increase is constant.

- That adding together the increasing and the decreasing costs yields a curve which decreases at first, reaches a minimum point and then starts to increase again.

- That the most economic batch quantity is the quantity

which corresponds to the minimum point on the combined cost curve.

Now it is true that this economic batch quantity (q) can be calculated from a simple formula:

$$q = \sqrt{\frac{2fs}{mr}}$$

where f is the fixed cost per set-up
s is the total units sold per annum
m is the variable manufacturing cost per unit
r is the rate of interest (expressed as a fraction)

It is not easy to explain why this formula is correct to a person who has no knowledge of differential calculus. To a reader who does understand calculus it is probably superfluous to point out that the formula above defines the point at which the differential coefficient of c (cost) with respect to q (quantity) is equal to zero, i.e. where q reaches its minimum value. This accounts for the square root sign. The 2 in the formula arises from the fact that the *average* stock is half the batch quantity ordered, assuming goods to be sold at a reasonably steady rate.

As a report writer it is not your task to include in the report a course in higher mathematics – even as an appendix! But the diagram in fact *is* an explanation and a perfectly adequate one for most purposes. In this case, and always assuming that the reader knows how to read a graph, the diagram gives immediate and almost total insight into the nature of the problem and is therefore, in these special circumstances, a more effective means of communication than either words or mathematical symbols. The diagram, and indeed any illustrative material, makes its impact because it is two-dimensional.

The eye takes in the whole picture at once. Language on the other hand is one-dimensional. The eye scans from left to right and, with practice, can take in a few words at a time but, in general, it takes much longer to absorb the information content of a thousand words than it does to assimilate the same amount of information presented graphically. Therefore do make use of diagrams. They can be very effective.

Presentation of statistical data

There are numerous ways in which it is possible to lie with statistics. Books have been written on the subject! Probably the most common type of statistical lie is a visual presentation in which an increase or a decrease in something is made to look more or less than it really is by playing tricks with the scale. For example, if you show an increase from 50 to 55 (i.e. an increase of ten per cent) but miss out part of the scale, starting from 25 instead of from zero, then what you have represented will *look* like an increase of 20 per cent.

Another typical lie is where general conclusions are drawn from data which relate to an unrepresentative sample. For example, you should not draw conclusions relating to all age groups and social classes from data obtained from a sample of university students or of psychiatric patients.

Assuming that your report is meant to give a true picture of the facts then you will not deliberately distort those facts. It is nevertheless important to be on your guard against the inadvertent misuse of statistical data. If you are not yourself a statistician then it may be wise to consult one in order to avoid one or other of the many pitfalls. A very common error is to draw a straight line through a scatter of points and thereby give the impression that there is a trend or correlation which in fact does not exist. Another common error is to fit a straight line through a scatter of points when the logically and mathematically correct line is some kind of curve. Perhaps the points should have been plotted on logarithmic graph paper before an attempt was made to fit a straight line to them. Having said that, the kind of chart in which one variable is plotted against another or against time is a very useful visual aid. The combination of a diagram, a table of figures and a verbal commentary is very powerful – so long as all three are neat and accurate. This kind of graph or time series is used to indicate trends in sales, production, consumption, population, etc. It is a convention that forecast trends and extrapolations are represented by dotted (or dashed) lines. An example of one of these graphs is given in Figure 2.4 which illustrates the decline in the use of horses and the growth in the use of tractors on farms in Great Britain. You do not have to be a statistician to draw the correct conclusion from this picture.

The pie chart is used to illustrate the proportions in which something is divided up. An example is given in Figure 2.5.

The bar chart is used to illustrate the comparative size of various quantities. The compound bar chart, which is really two or more bar charts combined into one, is used to show how two or more similar items (e.g. costs) vary with respect to each other as well as in some other dimension such as time. An example is Figure 2.6 which shows how, as a vehicle ages, the cost of maintenance increases while, at the same time, the cost of depreciation decreases. Putting the two costs together enables one to see how the total cost varies as the years go by and perhaps to draw

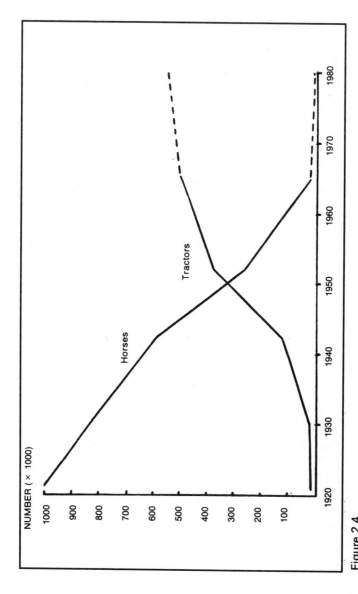

Figure 2.4
Graph showing number of horses and tractors used for agricultural purposes in Great Britain

33

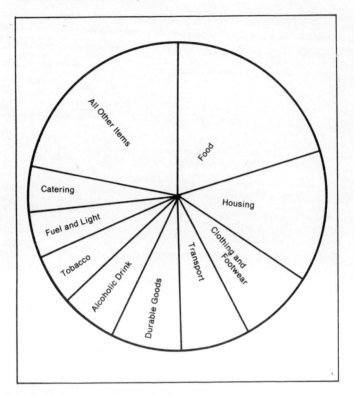

Figure 2.5
Pie chart showing consumers' expenditure

conclusions which might not be so obvious if each factor were to be considered separately.

The ideograph is a variant of the bar chart in which rows of little men (or cows, houses, tanks, aircraft, etc.), are used to represent quantities of these things. The method is not recommended for business reports because, apart from being difficult and time consuming, it is also a technique used to instruct schoolchildren and employees of low rank and can appear somewhat patronising. The

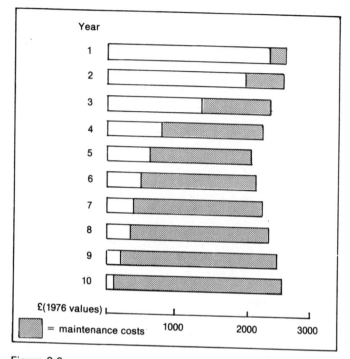

Figure 2.6
Bar chart showing depreciation and maintenance costs over ten years for a 32-ton gross articulated vehicle

ideograph which shows a picture of three-quarters of a cow, intended to represent 750 dairy cattle, may be more confusing than informative.

The histogram is used to represent the relative frequency or occurrence of a particular event or characteristic. The frequency polygon is used for the same purpose. The polygon is a closer approximation to the theoretical curve which describes the type of distribution to which the data belong. An example is given in Figure 2.7.

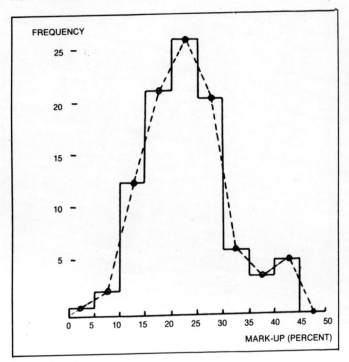

Figure 2.7
Frequency polygon showing distribution of mark-ups in the retailing of domestic electrical appliances

3

Layout

Every organisation which produces reports should establish a set of rules as to their layout. These rules are required (a) to ensure that all reports project the same 'brand image' (e.g. thoroughgoing professionalism or whatever is appropriate to the organisation), (b) to assist the author, the typist and the reader, all of whom will be able to work more easily and more efficiently if they get used to a particular style.

Inevitably, the rules are to some extent arbitrary. That is to say, there is not always a compelling reason why one rule rather than another should be followed. However, there are three basic factors to take into consideration before making a decision. The first is clarity: will it assist the reader's understanding? The second is appearance: will it make the typed page more pleasing to the eye? Remember that a neat and orderly page has a subliminal effect on the reader, predisposing him to think that the organisation which produced it is likewise neat and orderly and therefore reliable. The third is convenience: all other things being equal, you should select the method which involves the least effort and the least likelihood of error on the part of the typist. Above all, be consistent.

Margins

Margins are required for a number of very practical reasons. If there were no margins some of the text, on the left, would be obscured when the report was bound. Also, unless extreme care was taken some text on the right could be lost in the copying process. It is impossible not to leave a margin at the top of the page because of the way the paper fits into the typewriter, and some space has to be left at the foot of the page for the page numbers. Finally, in most reports, it is desirable to leave a certain amount of space for marginal notes.

A good rule, therefore, would be to leave an inch all round. However, if a binding method is used which takes up some space on the left, this should be allowed for. An extra quarter of an inch is usually sufficient. Also, on the first page of a chapter or of a major section of a report the upper margin should be bigger, say two inches. This space acts as a visual signal to the reader that he is about to embark on another stage in the discussion or presentation of facts. The report needs to be broken up in this way, particularly bearing in mind the fact that the reader may not be able to read it in a single session. Every gap in the text should be a suitable place to pause and such gaps should occur every few pages or, thinking in terms of reading time, every ten to fifteen minutes.

An exception to the one inch rule for the lower margin would sometimes have to be made at the end of the chapter to avoid having a final page with only one or two lines on it. One can either insert an extra line in the space normally allowed for the lower margin, or one can leave an extra wide margin on the penultimate page in order to ensure that there are three or four lines of print on the last page of the chapter. It is a matter which the typist should be able to decide.

If margins are too wide, i.e. if the area of print is too small, then the page will look wrong; it will look gimmicky or like a brochure with the illustrations missing. The reader will mistrust it. An A4 page is approximately 8¼ x 11¾ inches (21.0 x 29.7 centimetres). Margins of one inch (2.5 centimetres) all round gives a printed area of 63 per cent. Leaving margins twice as wide would result in a printed area of 34 per cent. Remembering that there are also indentations and spaces between paragraphs it is clear that wide margins place a severe restriction on the amount of information it is possible to present on one page. The reader would be forever turning over pages.

If a word processor is used it is possible to justify to the right as well as to the left, giving a very neat and professional appearance to the printed page. Some sophisticated typewriters also have the facility for justification to the right. If an ordinary typewriter is used then the paper guide and tabs can be set permanently to give the margins and indentations required. However, if the same typewriter is also used for producing a variety of letters and tables of figures on paper of more than one size, it may be helpful to prepare a sheet with the guidelines marked on it. This can be slipped behind the paper on which the text is to be typed and serve the double purpose of guide and backing sheet. An example of such a sheet is given in Figure 3.1.

Paragraphs

Some organisations have evolved extremely elaborate rules for dealing with various types of headings and subheadings, paragraphs and subparagraphs. However, there are sound practical reasons for preferring a relatively simple system. Many government reports and

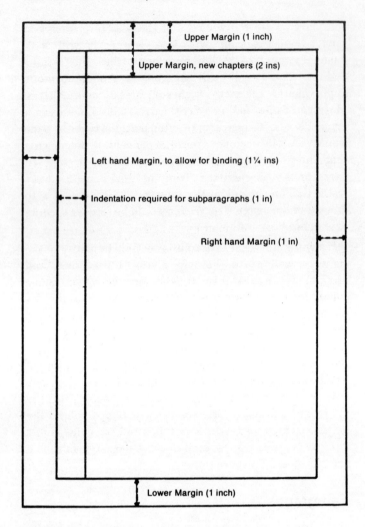

Upper Margin (1 inch)

Upper Margin, new chapters (2 ins)

Left hand Margin, to allow for binding (1¼ ins)

Indentation required for subparagraphs (1 in)

Right hand Margin (1 in)

Lower Margin (1 inch)

Figure 3.1
Guide sheet for report typist

other publications number the paragraphs straight through from beginning to end: 1, 2, 3, 4 ... etc. and use a totally separate and unrelated system for the chapters: I, II, III, IV ... etc. Using this system Chapter II, for example, could start with Paragraph 26, Chapter III with Paragraph 49, and so on. While this system has certain merits – it is certainly simple – it has the disadvantage that any alteration to the numbering of an early paragraph (e.g. as caused by the insertion of an extra paragraph) will necessitate changing all the subsequent paragraph numbers as well as a thorough check of all references in the text. This problem is largely obviated by using a two-part numbering system, i.e. numbering chapters 1, 2, 3 ... etc. and paragraphs within chapters 1.1, 1.2, 1.3 ... 2.1, 2.2, 2.3 ... etc. Using this system any renumbering takes place only within the chapter and does not affect other chapters which might well be being written by other authors.

Some organisations number paragraphs within sections and sections within chapters, using a three-part number: 1.1.1, 1.1.2, 1.1.3 ... etc. This principle can be pursued to absurd lengths and one has seen four-part and even five-part numbering systems. Such systems do not facilitate reference (which is the primary objective of a numbering system) and are therefore not recommended. The structure of a report should be clear and logical without any numbering system. The numbering system certainly should not be used to impose a structure on the report. This will lead only to confusion. Also, since it is normal to indent subparagraphs it follows that sub-subparagraphs should be further indented and, with a five-part system the first word, the first bit of useful information, would not appear until halfway across the page.

It has been noted that sometimes it is necessary to

include some subparagraphs within a paragraph. These may be labelled (1), (2), (3) . . . etc., particularly in the case of a list of recommendations or reasons for doing something. Alternatively, letters may be used: (a), (b), (c) . . . etc. Where there are only one or two subparagraphs within a paragraph or where there is a list not of sentences or clauses but of one, two or three-word items, then there is probably no need for any numbers or letters at all. Report writers should concentrate on writing clear English and not get carried away with the architecture of the reference frame. Have you ever seen a reference of the type 'Smith points out (Research Report 1234, III, 2 (a) (xviii)) . . .'? Probably not. On the other hand you may well have seen references of the type 'Smith points out in Research Report 1234 (para 3.2) . . .' Which is why a simple two-part numbering system is recommended.

As a general rule, sub-subparagraphs should be avoided. This can normally be achieved by having several short chapters rather than a few long chapters subdivided into major and minor sections.

There are two principal methods of typing numbered paragraphs. One is to 'block' the paragraphs and put the numbers in the margin. The other is to type the number as though it were the first word of the paragraph, that is, to indent it. The first method is preferable from the point of view of clarity and appearance. The second method makes for easier typing (because there is less tabbing) and is more economical on stationery. There may also be reports in which paragraphs need to be numbered unobtrusively rather than conspicuously, in the margin.

Where paragraphs are blocked it is of course necessary to leave a space between paragraphs. Where paragraphs are not blocked, that is, where the first line is indented, then it is not necessary but it is still desirable that a space should be left between paragraphs. Paragraphs help to break up a page of print; subparagraphs help to break up a long paragraph. All of this aids comprehension and looks more attractive than a page which is wholly covered in print.

Some report writers prefer to number sections and subsections of a report and to leave the actual paragraphs unnumbered. This makes a report look more like a book. It also makes precise references difficult. If individual paragraphs are not numbered then references can be given, as in a book, only by page and line number. Anyone looking up a reference by this method has actually to count the lines – which is tedious.

If chapters are numbered 1, 2, 3 ... etc. and if paragraphs within chapters are numbered 1.1, 1.2, 1.3 ... etc., then there is clearly no need to number sections, i.e. groups of paragraphs dealing with one particular subject within a more general chapter. Indeed, if sections were numbered 1.1, 1.2, 1.3 ... etc., then some other method of numbering paragraphs within sections would have to be found. This would be cumbersome and, in any case, superfluous.

Headings

The same argument which applies to paragraph numbering also applies to headings. Try to avoid the need for hierarchies of headings, subheadings, sub-subheadings, etc. This can be achieved by the same device of having short chapters (requiring headings) and sections (requiring subheadings). It may not be necessary to have any subdivision at all of a short chapter. However, if after having written an introductory paragraph you use a heading under which to discuss the first subject, the end of that section can be signalled only by a new heading. In other words, if a chapter is to be divided into sections then each section must deal with a particular subject and have its own subheading – even if some sections are only one paragraph long. The journalistic device of using key words or phrases to break up the text is not recommended for business reports. You do not wish to give the reader the impression that you are a slick wordmonger any more than you wish to give the impression that you are only semi-literate.

Chapter headings should be written in capitals, not underlined; section headings should be written in lower case, underlined. If the typewriter or word processor has a facility for producing a bold typeface then this may be used with advantage. There is no need to underline capitals since they are different anyway; the lower case subheadings should be underlined to distinguish them from the rest of the text. If subheadings could be italicised (as they usually are in books and periodicals) there would be no need to underline them.

Occasionally it is necessary to include a series of paragraphs each dealing with a particular subject within a section of a report. This is a case where subsection headings are required. The suggested method for dealing with this situation is to incorporate the subheading into the paragraph so that, as it were, the first word or phrase of the paragraph is the heading. This word or phrase should be underlined (or made bold or italicised).

Numbering of diagrams, tables and appendices

The recommended methods of chapter and paragraph numbering apply also to the numbering of diagrams, tables and appendices. Any diagrams or tables appearing within a chapter should be numbered consecutively, in the same way as the paragraphs, thus: Figure 1.1, Figure 1.2 . . ., Table 1.1, Table 1.2 . . . etc. Captions for diagrams and headings for tables should be treated as subheadings, i.e. lower case, underlined.

The way to deal with an appendix will to some extent depend on its length and form. If the appendix contains original material then it can be written in the same way as a chapter of the report. The paragraphs should be numbered consecutively 1, 2, 3 . . . etc. Often, however, an appendix includes various exhibits – copies of letters, computer output, extracts from other reports, and so on. In these cases it is best to provide an introductory page describing the material which is in the appendix and indicating the way in which it is to be identified. Perhaps the simplest way of dealing with this problem is to give each document its own appendix number and simply to list them in the table of contents. For example:

Appendix 1. Letter from Managing Director.
Appendix 2. Extract from Research Report No. 1234.
Appendix 3. Cash flow projection.
Appendix 4. Surveyor's report on North Factory.

Spacing

In deciding whether to use double spacing, single spacing or one-and-a-half spacing consideration should be given to the length and purpose of the report. Draft reports are normally double spaced. This leaves room to mark corrections and changes. Single spacing is recommended for long reports because it reduces the total number of pages. However, with single spacing, an effort should be made to ensure that paragraphs are fairly short and that a double space is left between paragraphs. This gives an attractive appearance to the page although the print is dense. For reports of average length, say, twenty to thirty pages, one-and-a-half spacing is recommended. Short subparagraphs should be single spaced but with double spaces between them. This ensures that each item within a list is isolated and therefore emphasised.

Tabular material should be arranged to fit the page in whatever way is best. In the first instance one should try to fit tables of figures within the margins which are used for the text. If there are more columns than will conveniently fit into the width of the page the following options may be considered:

- Turn the page on its side.
- Use a larger sheet of paper, folded in.
- Use a smaller type face.
- Type on a larger sheet of paper and reduce photographically.
- If there are many columns and few rows, transpose these and thus avoid the need to turn the page sideways.
- Make two small tables out of one large one.
- Give the table a double-page spread.

While is it clearly desirable that tables are typed using the normal typeface and can be read without having to turn the page on its side, statistics should never be doctored so that they fit into an available space. Nevertheless, if the number of digits can be kept down to three or four (by giving numbers in thousands or millions and by omitting superfluous decimal places) then it is quite feasible to get ten columns across the width of an A4 sheet. It is often the column heading rather than the numbers under the heading which determines the width of the column. It may therefore be convenient either to type the column headings sideways or simply to number the columns and give the key at the foot of the page.

When to print on both sides of the paper

Reports are normally produced using one side of the paper only. This is because with the normal type of photocopying equipment it takes longer to print on both sides of the paper and there is a greater risk of spoiling some of the pages, getting them out of sequence and so on. Nevertheless it is obviously more economical to print on both sides of the sheet and, in the case of lengthy reports there are distinct advantages in cutting down the weight and thickness of the document. With short reports the opposite argument applies. A ten-page document sandwiched between two attractive covers is a report. Four sheets of paper, closely typed on both sides and stapled together looks like a tedious memorandum from a Scrooge. The information content of the two documents might be exactly the same. The effect could be very different.

Even when a report is printed on one side only, some pages may need to be printed on both sides. The table of figures spread across two pages has already been mentioned. There is also the case of a diagram which needs to be viewed alongside the relevant text. A double-page spread cannot satisfactorily be achieved if the sheets are printed on one side only, because it leaves the two preceding pages blank, and this tends to look like a mistake.

Summary

Experience has taught that in normal circumstances the following rules work very well:

- Margins: about one inch all round.
- Paragraphs: blocked, numbered consecutively within chapters 1.1, 1.2, 1.3 . . . etc.
- Headings: chapters – capitals; sections – lower case, underlined.
- Spacing: one-and-a-half; single spacing for sub-paragraphs.
- Try to avoid: sub-subparagraphs, sub-subheadings, tables with over ten columns.
- Try to be consistent but recognise that occasionally it may be desirable to break one of the rules.

An example which illustrates most of these points is given in Figure 3.2.

1. SUMMARY

1.1 The Company currently manufactures television sets using two systems. One system, used for production of the A20 series is to be phased out; the other more highly mechanised system, used for production of the B30 series, is to be retained. A new series (the C40) is to be introduced and will replace the A20 series. The production methods to be used for the C40 will be the same as for the B30. However, while the two production lines in the reorganised factory will be similar, there will be numerous other changes related to the flow of materials which will have to be made and these changes will affect the efficiency and cost of the whole operation. It is therefore necessary to ensure that, in the new layout of the factory, stores, plant and equipment are located in such a manner as to minimise materials handling costs.

Terms of reference

1.2 The Group Work Study Department was asked to consider this problem, paying particular attention to two cost centres, namely, Manufacturing Overhead (Stores) and Direct Labour Excesses (Handling). It was agreed that the study would:

(1) Identify specific costs related to the movement of materials and assemblies.

(2) Compare costs relevant to alternative locations of production facilities.

(3) Provide reliable information for future changes in manufacturing methods.

1.3 It was further agreed that the Work Study team should spend the first week making a brief survey of the whole problem and that..........

Figure 3.2
Example of report page layout

4

Language

The particular way in which an author puts his sentences together, his choice of words, his use of certain conventions, add up to his style. There is no unique style which is ideally suited to report writing since reports themselves necessarily vary, depending on the subject matter and the purpose for which the report has been written. Nevertheless, certain principles are generally applicable. H. W. Fowler, author of *Modern English Usage* and of *The King's English,* advised that one should:

- Prefer the familiar word to the far-fetched.
- Prefer the concrete word to the abstract.
- Prefer the single word to the circumlocution.
- Prefer the short word to the long.
- Prefer the Saxon word to the Romance.

Sir Arthur Quiller Couch in *The Art of Writing* disagreed with the last two of these precepts on the ground that there must be a very large number of justifiable exceptions. His rules were:

- Almost always prefer the concrete word to the abstract.
- Almost always prefer the direct word to the circumlocution.

- Generally use transitive verbs in the active voice.
- Be sparing in the use of adjectives.

Sir Ernest Gowers in *The Complete Plain Words* provides three rules:

- Avoid the superfluous word.
- Choose familiar words.
- Choose precise words.

So far as report writing is concerned all this worthy advice can be distilled down to one simple injunction: be clear, concise and correct. If your writing can be described by these three adjectives then, it goes without saying, you will have avoided all the worst pitfalls. You will have used familiar words, direct words, short words; you will have avoided ambiguity, 'loaded' words, clichés, jargon, figures of speech, superfluous words, tautologies, split infinitives, double negatives, non-sequiturs, sentences which end with prepositions.

Familiar words. Why should one prefer the familiar word to the unusual? Because it is more likely that the reader will know and understand the familiar word. Time is short and he does not want to be continually looking up words in the dictionary. On the other hand it may be necessary to introduce the reader to a technical term or to some other unfamiliar word in order to avoid being long-winded. In these circumstances the technical term or unfamiliar word should be defined in the text before any discussion takes place. This will save the reader from having to look up the word and it will avoid any further explanations or circumlocutions which might otherwise be necessary. Apart from words which have different meanings in different contexts (e.g. 'variance' which means one thing to an accountant and another to a statistician) there are several apparently familiar words (e.g. 'efficiency' and 'productivity') which also need to be qualified and/or defined the first time they are used since they are liable to be misinterpreted. Thus, if 'productivity' is used in a report to signify 'labour productivity' and 'labour productivity' is defined as 'effective output per man-hour' then this needs to be said at least once.

Concrete words. Why should one (almost always) prefer the concrete word to the abstract? Because there is no argument about the meaning of a concrete noun, taken in its context. Nearly all abstract nouns are vague and therefore open to misunderstanding. People tend to use abstract words and expressions in order to avoid saying something more specific.

Transitive verbs. Why should one generally use transitive verbs in the active voice? Because this construction forces you to specify who does what. A passive construction enables you to conceal the identity of the doer of the deed and this in turn suggests that you are either ignorant or disingenuous. The fact is that sentences of the form subject-verb-object convey more information in fewer words than any other construction. However, it is not possible to use the active voice all the time and sometimes it may be desirable to use the passive voice in order to avoid excessive use of personal pronouns (which will be discussed later in this chapter) and words such as 'the team', 'the authors' or 'your investigator'. As a general guide at least 50 per cent of verbs should be in the active voice. If too few verbs are active the effect is to slow down the narrative, conveying less information with more words. If too many verbs are active the result is 'action-packed' or very dynamic prose which may be inappropriate in a business report. The same remarks apply to transitive and intransitive verbs. Transitive verbs, which take a direct object, speed up the action.

Ambiguity can be amusing, annoying or misleading. Amusing examples, particularly those perpetrated by politicians and civil servants, are frequently and gleefully quoted in the press. Ambiguity can be caused by putting words in the wrong order, by incorrect punctuation and by the use of pronouns which could refer either to the subject or the object. For example, 'A met B and he gave him a message'. The word 'only' should precede the word or phrase it qualifies. Thus 'I go there only on Fridays' means 'I do not go there on any other day' whereas 'I only go there on Fridays' strictly implies 'I go there but do not come back on Fridays' (although only a lawyer or possibly a foreign student might be inclined to read it in this way).

Loaded words (words which prejudice the reader) are out of place in a business report. Words such as 'ridiculous' and 'amazing' should obviously be avoided and even words like 'unscientific' and 'illogical' should be treated with caution.

A **cliché** is a hackneyed phrase which has become trite by overuse. At the same time a cliché may be no more than a colourful way of disguising ignorance. What do you really mean when you talk about a 'can of worms' or of 'creatures coming out of the woodwork'?

Jargon (the technical vocabulary of a particular profession or field of study), should generally be avoided unless the report is being written primarily to inform (or impress?) members of that profession. Management, however, is a broadly based discipline. Therefore the specialised terms of, say, the statistician or the social scientist should be avoided. If it is essential that a technical term should be used (e.g. to save a whole paragraph of explanation) then, as mentioned in connection with the use of familiar words, that term should be defined on the first occasion that it is used.

Figures of speech such as hyperbole (exaggerated statement) and metaphor are generally out of keeping with the style of a serious business document. In a report one does not leave no stone unturned, one undertakes a thorough search. The precise interpretation of a colourful phrase may be open to doubt, and mixed metaphors especially can be very distracting. It is better to say exactly what you mean in the first place.

Superfluous words and phrases are more of a hindrance than a help. They waste everybody's time and raise doubts in the reader's mind as to the writer's intentions. Is he perhaps trying to disguise the fact that he has very little to say by wrapping it up in a mass of verbiage? When simple words are available there is no good reason why much longer phrases should be used, for example:

- in order to (= to)
- in view of this fact (= so)
- in the event that (= if)
- at the present time (= now)
- on the occasion of (= when)

Tautology is saying the same thing twice with different

words in the same sentence. An example from a report on a meeting is 'The extreme brevity of the notice given was far too short'. Tautologies, liked mixed metaphors, should be avoided.

Split infinitives. There appear to be two reasons why one should not split an infinitive and neither of them is very convincing. The first is that people will think you are ignorant – an impression which you do not wish to give. The second is that in some other languages such as French and Latin the infinitive cannot be split because it is only one word. In English, however, the infinitive nearly always consists of two words. (In certain instances the 'to' is omitted, e.g. after 'can' or 'should'.) If the operative word is separated from its 'to' by an adverb, does this really matter? Is it not possible that the verb and the qualifying adverb might go together to form one single idea? If so, then surely it might be just as wrong to separate these two words as to split the infinitive. The same argument applies to phrases such as 'not quite' and 'only just'. Consider the three possible positions for 'not quite' in conjunction with 'to reach your objective'. You can say (a) 'not quite to reach your objective', (b) 'to reach your objective not quite' or (c) 'to not quite reach your objective'. Of the three the split infinitive is to be preferred because 'not quite reach' has the force of a single word even though it is actually three words. 'Overreach' is one word and one would not dream of splitting it. There are evidently occasions when it is better to split than not to split and, equally, there are occasions when infinitives should not be split. If you want a rule, then this is it: an infinitive may be split if and only if the qualifying adverb or phrase is very closely associated with the verb. This might apply to 'barely', 'almost', etc., but not to expressions such as 'except on rare occasions', 'meticulously', etc. It is a matter of euphony rather than grammar.

Double negatives logically cancel each other out. 'Not never' means 'sometimes'. Therefore, if you wish to emphasise a negative this cannot be achieved by repetition. Some other device must be used. Double negatives are not to be confused with litotes – a means of expressing an affirmative by the negative of its contrary, for example, 'not inconsiderable' or 'not inconceivable'. The latter, used sparingly, is an acceptable device.

A non sequitur is a conclusion which does not logically follow from what has previously been stated. In practice most non sequiturs are due to faulty expression rather than faulty reasoning. The writer has two unconnected statements to make but instead of letting them stand as two separate sentences he connects them with an 'and' or an 'although' or a 'whilst' thereby creating a non sequitur. The reader will be puzzled. He may think he is looking at a sentence in which there is a misprint or in which a phrase has been omitted. An example is: 'We have several staff who are professionally qualified to deal with this kind of problem and George Smith is resident in your area.' (The writer should have said: *including* George Smith who lives in your area.')

Sentences ending with prepositions. It is possible to avoid ending sentences with prepositions but sometimes the alternative construction is so awkward that it is better to disobey the rule concerning prepositions. Winston Churchill is alleged to have made the marginal comment on a memorandum from one of his civil servants:

'This is the kind of nonsense up with which I will not put.' The point is that there are numerous verbs which are formed by adding one or two prepositions to a simple verb; 'put' and 'put up with' is a good example. The problem can be avoided by using a different word – 'tolerate'. But Fowler says we should prefer the Saxon word to the Romance! The best advice which can be given on this subject therefore must be that there can be no harm in ending sentences with prepositions. Indeed, there is no logical reason why this construction should be avoided. On the other hand, too frequent use can be annoying.

Language is continually changing and developing and words may now be used correctly in ways which would have been considered incorrect ten or twenty years ago. The English language is spoken all over the world and the same words have different meanings in different places. Thus 'enjoin' in the UK generally means 'instruct' or 'command' whereas in the USA it usually means 'prohibit' or 'prevent'. The dictionary gives both meanings. The dictionary (Concise Oxford Dictionary, New Edition, first published 1976) now accepts 'hopefully' as meaning 'it is hoped that' whereas until recently this usage would have been regarded as incorrect. Reports and official writing generally are conservative in style and it is better to leave the coining of new words to journalists or writers of fiction and wait until they have been thoroughly absorbed into everyday use before incorporating them into reports. There are a number of words which are so frequently used in one sense that the significance of their original, correct meaning may be lost on the reader. It is a strange paradox that the correct use of a word may well lead to a misunderstanding because the reader is in the habit of using the word in some other sense. Nevertheless, it cannot be wrong to use a word correctly whereas to use a word in a way that the reader was probably taught at school that it should not be used can only lead to annoyance. Do not use a word such as 'anticipate' or 'accept' unless it is quite clear from the context which of its two or more possible meanings is intended. Say 'expect' or 'forestall' instead of 'anticipate'; say 'recognise' or 'agree' for 'accept'. Then there will be no ambiguity. Other words which can cause similar difficulties are:

- *Apparent*. This is not the same as 'evident'. To say that something is apparent contains the implication that it may not be real. Appearances can be deceptive whereas evidence is supposed to be conclusive.

- *Basic*. This means 'fundamental'. It may incidentally be simple but the word 'basic' does not mean 'simple'.

- *Effective*. This does not mean the same as 'efficient'. An operation is effective if the objective is achieved. It is efficient if it is achieved with the minimum of effort. You can measure efficiency on a scale from, say, 0 to 100, but effectiveness is a 'go/no go' measure.

- *Essential*. If something is 'essential' it means it is 'indispensable'. This is more than just important.

A discipline which is sometimes recommended is to go through a piece of writing and cross out all the adjectives. Then you go back and reinstate only those adjectives which are absolutely necessary. The same might be said of adverbs. The following is a short list of adjectives (and there are corresponding adverbs) which are frequently used when, upon analysis, it will be found that they either add nothing which has not already been said or, sometimes, distort the meaning of what has been said.

- Absolute
- Actual
- Essential
- Massive
- Primary
- Real
- Utter
- Vital

If a word is obviously redundant as in the phrase 'utterly and completely' or 'completely empty' (bearing in mind that 'complete' means 'full'!) miss it out. If an adjectival or adverbial phrase can be reduced to a single word then reduce it. The aim in report writing is to be clear, concise and correct, to persuade by means of logic and not by means of fine sounding phrases and rhetorical devices. 'It is obvious that' means 'obviously', but if it *is* obvious then it is *obvious*, and there is no need to point it out. 'In the first place' means 'firstly'. However, in a report, if you are going to list several reasons for doing something or examples of something then it is perhaps easier to number them (1), (2), (3), etc., instead of constructing a rambling paragraph starting with 'First and foremost' and ending with 'Last but not least'.

Difficulties sometimes arise with the use of the conditional tense. Do not say 'would' if you mean 'will' or 'do'. 'We would advise ...' implies that there is an 'if' or a 'but' to follow and that, actually, 'we advise something different'. Further difficulties arise with the confusion of 'will' and 'shall', 'would' and 'should':

- 'I will do it' means 'I want and intend to do it'.
- 'I shall do it' means, 'It will be done by me (in the future)'.
- 'You will do it' means 'It will be done by you (in the future)'.
- 'You shall do it' means 'I am ordering you to do it'.

- 'I would do it' implies that I should like to do it but for some reason I cannot.

- 'I should do it' implies that I ought to do it but for some reason I cannot.

- 'You would do it' implies that something is preventing you from doing it.

- 'You should do it' implies that it is your duty to do it.

First person 'shall' is the future tense, first person 'will' implies volition. Second person 'will' is the future tense, second person 'shall' implies obligation. The English language can be confusing but, on the other hand, when it is used correctly different shades of meaning can be conveyed very efficiently, using fewer and shorter words than would be needed in other languages. The meaning of 'should' should be clear from the context. Should it not be clear then some alternative construction should be used. Obligation can always be expressed by 'ought', necessity by 'must'.

'May' and 'might' can be interchangeable in some contexts. Collins Cobuild Dictionary, which was specially developed for learners and teachers of English, gives the same initial definition for both words. 'When you say that something may (or might) happen or be true you mean that it will possibly happen or be true in the future, but you cannot be certain.' Strictly, 'may' and 'might' are both parts of the same (defective) verb. 'May' in the present tense and 'might' in the past tense both mean 'let'. Thus 'may I speak?' means 'will you let me speak?' or 'do I have your permission to speak?' 'May' in the future tense and 'might' in the conditional tense mean 'can' and 'could' respectively. There is not much real difference but 'may' can imply a higher probability than 'might'. Thus 'I may well' have done something means 'I probably did do it' whereas 'I might well' have done something usually means that (for some reason or other) 'I probably did not do it.'

Writers of reports and of technical and learned articles are frequently instructed not to use the first person and sometimes also not to use the second person but to keep the narrative entirely impersonal. The principal objection to 'we' appears to be that it can be ambiguous. It can stand for the authors of the report or the people who did the work which is the subject of the report or it can mean I, the author and you, the reader. It is possible to say 'the author and his colleagues' instead of 'we' but I think that, having stated once who 'we' are, subsequent references are not likely to be ambiguous, particularly if you are careful not to use 'we' in the sense of 'anyone'. In fact, it is better to use 'you' in this sense than 'we'. 'You' is the usual method of implying 'anyone' in everyday speech and it is generally obvious from the context that 'you' means 'one' and not you personally. This is not a letter and I do not know who will be reading it. There is nothing wrong with 'one' but excessive use of 'one' does get on one's nerves. Excessive use of any word or phrase can be annoying and a good report writer will ring the changes: sometimes he will specify his subject as 'the Company', 'the Management' or whatever; sometimes he will say 'we' and sometimes he will turn the sentence round and use a passive construction. To further amplify this discussion two letters are quoted below; in the first one a writer objects to being told by an editor that he must write in the third person and in the second one the editor explains why, in his view, contributors to his journal should write in the third person.

It has just been noticed that in the May 1980 issue of

the Journal of the OR Society, instruction 4 to contributors was changed from 'Avoid the use of footnotes' to 'Papers should be written in the third person without the use of footnotes'. No attention was drawn to the change either in the Journal or elsewhere. It is possible to conjecture as to the reasons for this amendment.

Earlier this year a refereed paper was returned to an author with the comment 'We do not publish papers in the first person'. The referee then wrote to Prof. Haley pointing out that no such policy was mentioned in the instructions and that it was not reasonable to have unwritten policies of this type. No doubt this explains the change in instructions, but why does such a policy exist? Who authorised it? Have Council ever considered the matter?

The writer is at a loss to understand the objection to the first person. The purpose of a journal is to communicate, and formality of style should be subordinated to clarity and ease of understanding. Authors write most lucidly in the style which comes naturally to them. If some find the first person comes easily, so be it. It is arrogant and unnecessary to insist otherwise. The sole criteria should be clarity and intelligibility ...

Reply

We (my editorial assistant and I) replied to Dr. Sasieni's original letter to explain our (royal) reasons for insisting on the third person. It is quite easy in the course of an oral presentation for us (the audience) to distinguish when we (the speaker) are referring to our (the author's) experience or our (the audience and speaker's) beliefs of our (human beings') requirements.

With the written word, however, our (the writer's) emphasis is blurred, and we (the readers) can often be confused when we (readers/authors/society/society members) believe we (?) understand. If we (members of past Councils) had wished to control our (editors') policy and our (the Society's) publications, then we (members) would not have approved our (the Publications Committee's) terms of reference.

Our journal succeeds because of the efforts of our members and friends. We are fortunate in having our newsletter where we can air this matter and we are grateful to our editor for giving us our opportunity without questioning our decision on our policy.

It is not enough to use all the right words. These words must be strung together into sentences which are grammatically correct and easy to understand. It is good advice to report writers to tell them that their sentences should generally be short. However, if a report is to be lively and interesting then sentences should be of mixed length: some short (up to ten words), some of middling length (ten to twenty words) and, occasionally, a long one. Aim for an average length of between fifteen and twenty words but remember that the span, that is the difference between the longest and the shortest sentence may reasonably be as much as thirty words. A sentence is defined *(Concise Oxford Dictionary*, 6th edition, 1976) as a 'set of words complete in itself as expression of thought, containing subject and predicate (either, or part of either or both, of which may be omitted by ellipsis), and conveying a statement, question, exclamation or command'. The end of a sentence is marked by the appropriate punctuation mark.

Here is what looks like a long sentence, taken from an

actual report. It is, in fact, two compound sentences, separated by a semicolon:

> The problem typically facing laundries is one of inadequate throughput with, in consequence, high unit costs and so long as this situation prevails improvements in productivity can make a marginal contribution only; better pay means higher prices, and this in turn means more laundry closures.

The two parts of the first sentence are connected by 'and'. However, it is clear that 'and' is the wrong connecting word. It would be better to omit the conjunction altogether and make two separate sentences. The first sentence is pompous and verbose. 'Typically' is wrongly used to qualify 'facing'. 'Marginal contribution' is accountants' jargon and the meaning would be obscure to many readers of the report. And when the author wrote 'prevails' he almost certainly meant to write 'persists'. The second sentence uses short and punchy words. 'Better pay means higher prices' sounds like an advertising slogan, as if higher prices were desirable. Sudden changes of style are generally inappropriate in business reports. A rewritten version of this passage makes use of five short sentences and maintains a consistent style:

> The problem facing many laundries today is that they cannot get enough work. Consequently unit costs are high. In this situation improvements in labour productivity can make little impact on costs. Therefore, if pay is increased, prices will also have to be increased. Then fewer people will make use of laundries and more laundries will close.

The secret to remember when constructing long

sentences is to keep the various parts of the sentence (subordinate clauses, parentheses, etc.), in a logical order, so that the sentence flows. In a short sentence it can be effective to put the words in an unusual order or to produce a convoluted sentence. You can get away with 'When you have finished, let me know' although 'Let me know when you have finished' is preferable. What you should not do is write as follows: 'Although "Let me know when you have finished" is preferable to "When you have finished, let me know', you can get away with it. That kind of sentence is difficult to follow. It is not absolutely clear what 'it' is.

A second piece of advice concerning long sentences is to use well known constructions so that the reader knows what to expect. 'Not only' will be followed in due course by 'but also' so do not surprise and confuse the reader by throwing in 'and furthermore' as an afterthought. If you are constructing a sentence with three 'whether' or 'that' clauses it may be helpful to the reader to let him know what is coming and then, for extra clarity, actually number the clauses. The following example is taken from a report on a price survey:

The three most common types of error are: (1) where the object has the wrong label, (2) where the object has the wrong price and/or the wrong description, (3) where there is a copying error in one or more figures or letters, e.g. 'GB' copied as '613'.

Incidentally, do not hesitate to use 'and/or' if that is what you mean. One small deficiency in the English language is that it does not have two different words for 'or' depending on whether the alternatives are mutually exclusive (*aut* in Latin) or the difference between them is unimportant (*vel* in Latin).

Sometimes the subject matter is complicated and difficult to explain. The report writer has to be careful not to pack too much information into one paragraph, making unwarranted assumptions about the reader's knowledge and understanding of the subject. He also has to be careful not to burden the reader with masses of unnecessary detail. Tell the reader all but no more than he needs to know. Do not 'blind him with science' and do not try to impress him with the amount of work you have done. It is the quality, not the quantity which counts.

The following is an example of how, after several attempts, a difficult section of a report was handled. It was a report to a senior executive – someone who trusted his advisers sufficiently not to want to check all the arithmetic and who did not require detailed instruction in the particular techniques used.

The Region is currently served by one depot in the South. The weekly schedule for vehicles based at this depot involves:

- 30 hours driving at an average speed of 25 mph (= 750 miles)

- 8 hours unloading goods

- 10 hours allowances (depot, meals, etc.)

If the Region were divided and served by two depots, one in the North and one in the South, then vehicles would be able to make more trips: less time would be spent driving and fewer vehicles would be needed to deliver the same quantity of goods.

An exercise was undertaken in which the two-depot operation was simulated. Data for the Southern depot was obtained from existing records. Data for the hypothetical Northern depot was obtained using distances from the route planning map.

In the schedule for this two-depot situation the time per week for the average vehicle was:

- 25.5 hours driving at an average speed of 25 mph (= 637.5 miles)

- 12.5 hours unloading goods

- 10.0 hours allowances (depot, meals, etc.)

The extra 4.5 hours of unloading time represents an increase of 56 per cent in the amount of goods which the average vehicle would deliver in a week. Also, since the mileage covered would be reduced from 750 to 637.5 per week, vehicle running costs would be reduced by 15 per cent. Standing costs per vehicle would remain the same but the total number of vehicles required would be reduced from 26 to 19.

One final comment on long sentences: if you are constructing a sentence with two or more clauses, try to write it so that the clauses are roughly the same shape and length. It will then have balance and rhythm which make for easy reading and comprehension.

A paragraph may be described as a unit of thought, that is, it is a sentence or a set of sentences which contains one idea or one argument. At the same time a paragraph is also an aesthetic device which is used to break up a page of print and allow you to pause, if necessary, in the middle of a complex argument. From an aesthetic point of view, it is desirable that the paragraphs within a report should be fairly short, so that there can be three or four to a page. If logic demands a long paragraph it can still be broken up by the inclusion of an indented sub-paragraph or list. This makes for easier reading and better understanding.

5

Spelling and punctuation

The previous chapter was concerned with words, sentences and paragraphs. These are the building blocks of language. In this chapter the discussion is about the letters or symbols used to represent words and about the punctuation marks and other devices which, if you like, represent the mortar between the bricks.

Spelling

Spelling is an emotional subject. Some people say that words ought to be spelt as they are pronounced and that, so long as the meaning is clear, it should not matter whether the spelling is correct. Some people have never learned to spell correctly and do not take the time to look words up in a dictionary. Whatever the reasons for bad spelling (blame it on bad teaching, blame it on laziness), the fact is that the reader is likely to notice it and make unfortunate inferences about the writer. A professional writer or printer is not expected to make mistakes and there is a limit to the number of errors which can be tolerated even in a non-professional. The limit is about one mistake per ten pages, after checking. After having gone through the processes of drafting, typing, revising, checking, retyping and checking again, there is really no excuse for mistakes. The odd mistake will nearly always get through, but take extra care in spelling names and addresses and ensure that the first page of anything you write is free from error.

There are two basic rules for spelling. First, if you are not sure, look it up in the dictionary; second, if there is more than one spelling of a word (e.g. 'spelt' and 'spelled') make your mind up as to which alternative you prefer and stick to it. By remembering 'i before e except after c', you will be able to spell words like 'believe' and 'conceive'; but beware of exceptions to this rule such as 'freight', 'foreign', 'height' and 'seize'. Also, some of the rules relating to the doubling of consonants are so complicated that it is probably easier just to learn the correct spelling for each word.

Some commonly mis-spelt words are:

abbreviate	dissatisfied
accommodate	embarrass
argument	gauge
asphalt	inoculate
awful	mischievous
consensus	separate
courtesy	skilful
crystalline	superintendent
definite	supersede
desiccated	tenancy
disappear	unparalleled
disastrous	variegated

There are many words which may be spelt in two different ways. Words ending in '-ise' or '-ize' form a large group. Sometimes there is no '-ize' alternative (as in 'advertise', 'enterprise', 'supervise', 'surprise'); the safe rule, therefore, is always to use '-ise'. Other words where alternatives exist are:

biased/biassed
connection/connexion
despatch/dispatch
enquiry/inquiry
focusing/focussing

Finally there are a number of words which are almost the same but which have different meanings. It is important that the correct spelling is used because the majority of well educated readers will notice when the incorrect word is used and it will bother them. Confusion of 'principal' (meaning 'main') and 'principle (meaning 'general rule') is very common. A person whose title or appointment includes the word 'Principal' would find it very difficult to forgive this confusion. Other pairs of words which are often confused are:

alternate (e.g. ABABAB...)
alternative (e.g. A or B)
complementary (making a whole)
complimentary (speaking well of)
dependant (noun)
dependent (adjective)
forego (precede, as in 'foregone conclusion')
forgo (go without)
licence (noun)
license (verb)
stationary (not moving)
stationery (paper, writing materials)

A knowledge of Latin or Greek often gives a clue as to the spelling of a word. For example, *ante* means 'before' as in 'anteroom' or 'antecedent'; *anti* means 'against' as in 'anticlimax' or 'antiseptic'.

The spelling of most English words became established in the seventeenth century when the first dictionaries were published. Samuel Johnson's famous dictionary was completed in 1755. Language, including spelling and pronunciation, continues to evolve; for instance, 'night is still pronounced 'nicht' in Scotland while the American spelling 'nite' is currently gaining ground, but this is no excuse for inconsistency from day to day and from person to person within an organisation.

Punctuation

Punctuation marks serve two purposes: rhetorical and logical. They tell you where to pause: for breath if you are talking, for thought if you are reading. And they help you overcome ambiguity. Some legal documents are drafted in such a way that commas are not necessary because, it is argued, the omission of a necessary comma can radically alter the meaning of a sentence. A sentence in a legal document may contain a long succession of 'whereas' clauses and go on for three pages before the main verb is reached, making it almost totally incomprehensible.

There is one simple rule relating to punctuation: do not insert a comma or any other punctuation mark unless it is necessary, whether for rhetorical or logical reasons. Consistency in use of punctuation marks is important. Having decided, for instance, that lists should be preceded by a colon, do not introduce the use of any other device, such as a dash or a colon and a dash.

The four principal punctuation marks or stops are, in ascending order of magnitude, the comma, the semicolon, the colon and the full stop. They represent pauses in speech or thought. The gap between the end of one paragraph and the beginning of the next may be regarded, from a rhetorical point of view, as a fifth and longer type of pause. Question marks and exclamation marks are usually the equivalent of full stops. Placed in brackets in the middle of a sentence a question mark can mean 'this needs checking' and an exclamation mark may mean 'you may not believe this but it is actually true'.

A full stop may be used to mark the end of a sentence but all sentences do not necessarily end with a full stop or a question mark or an exclamation mark. A list of short and similar sentences may be separated by semicolons or even commas only.

Full stops are also used after initials or abbreviations, but they need not be. Typists are currently taught to miss out the full stops after initials because they are not necessary. Thus, 'J E Smith OBE' is neater and quicker to write or type than 'J. E. Smith, O.B.E.'. Again, the important rule is to be consistent. You must not write 'U.K.' in one sentence and 'USA' in the next. Three full stops (or dots) in a row are used to indicate the omission of part of a quotation.

Colons are normally used in front of lists, even if there are only two items in the list. A colon divides a sentence where both parts are grammatically complete in themselves, e.g.: 'I am going to tell you something: this is it.' A semicolon is normally used to separate the items in a list where each item could form a sentence in itself. Thus: 'I am going to tell you three things: this is one; this is another; this is the third.' For complex lists, e.g. a set of recommendations, the following guidelines may be followed:

(a) Each recommendation should be written out as a sub-paragraph.

(b) Each subparagraph should start with a capital letter and finish with a full stop.

Commas are normally used to separate short items in a

list, and their absence can lead to misinterpretation as in a list of the type 'Woolworths, Littlewoods, and Marks and Spencers'. However, there is no need to insert commas between adjectives in phrases such as 'a large articulated lorry' because there could not be any ambiguity. 'However' meaning 'but' is followed by a comma or has commas around it if in the middle of a sentence. 'However' meaning 'in whatever way' is not followed by a comma.

A comma is used in a complex sentence to separate clauses; commas are also used to isolate a phrase from the rest of the sentence. Sometimes a problem arises where, in order to make the sense absolutely clear, a pair of commas is logically required within another pair of commas. There are several ways of getting round this problem. One is to rewrite the sentence so as to avoid it. Another is to substitute brackets or dashes for one of the pairs of commas. Brackets or dashes (make up your mind which you prefer) are frequently used to mark a parenthesis within the sentence. Commas may be used for the same purpose, particularly in the case of phrases such as 'to the best of my knowledge and belief'. A parenthesis which is grammatically complete in itself, such as 'make up your mind which you prefer', is probably best placed between brackets.

Quotation marks

Quotation marks can be either double or single. You can use double quotation marks except for quotations within quotations, for which you will use single quotation marks. Or vice versa. But be consistent. On some typewriters the single quotation mark is the same as the apostrophe and this can also be used over a full stop to form an exclamation mark. On this kind of typewriter the double quotation mark is higher than the apostrophe and it is the double quotation mark which is clearly meant to be used for quotations. The use of inverted commas seems to have disappeared, almost certainly because it is more efficient and more useful to have only one key on the typewriter for quotation marks. Inverted commas were originally used to mark the beginning of a quotation. Now, the same sign is used both at the beginning and the end of the quotation.

Remember that if a quotation forms only part of a sentence the quotation mark may be followed by a stop. If on the other hand the quotation forms the whole sentence then the stop will come before the quotation mark. The same rule applies to brackets. Where the whole sentence is parenthesised, the stop is placed inside the brackets. If only the last word or phrase is in brackets, the stop is placed outside. If a sentence ends with a quotation within a quotation then both quotation marks (double and single) should be given, the one following the other. But if a sentence ends with the end of a quoted sentence, implying the need for two stops, one after the other, then the convention is to omit the second stop. 'The man shouted "Help!"' Not 'The man shouted "Help!".'. The same applies to abbreviations: write 'etc'. and not 'etc..' at the end of a sentence.

Hyphens

Hyphens are used (a) to join words together and (b) to split words. But what is a word? Consider the following: 'windmill', 'water-mill', 'cotton mill'. They are all correct. Pairs of words like 'cotton mill' and hyphenated words like 'water-mill' may one day become single words like 'windmill' – language is evolving all the time. It is advisable to use the dictionary to discover the currently accepted spelling. Words like 'mis-spell' and 'trans-ship' are hyphenated apparently because of the way in which they are pronounced; the same applies to 'co-operate' and 'co-ordinate'. Occasionally a hyphen may be used to distinguish between two different meanings and pronunciations of what would otherwise be the same word. For example, 'recover' means 'rescue' whereas 're-cover' means 'replace the cover'.

If a word has to be split because there is not enough space for all of it on the same line, the break should be made between syllables. Examples are: 'con-flicting' or 'conflict-ing', 'over-throw', 'wind-mill', 'other-wise'. Monosyllables and some longer words such as 'enough' and 'apple', cannot be split.

The most difficult problems of hyphenation arise with words which can be written with or without a hyphen. The best rule seems to be to use a hyphen where the meaning might otherwise be different or ambiguous. Thus two-figure numbers ('twenty-one', 'two-thirds', etc.) should be hyphenated because each part could represent a single quantity. 'Two thirds ' might mean two separate portions each equal to one third of the whole (compare 'two halves'). It might also mean 'two third places' in a competition. Similarly, adjectival phrases such as 'red-hot' (as in 'red-hot poker') should be hyphenated since not to do so would be to alter the meaning. Long-winded phrases such as 'never-to-be-forgotten day' and 'under-the-counter transaction' can usually be avoided by recasting the sentence so that it sounds more like English and less like German (in which language composite words of the form 'nevertobeforgotten' are frequently to be found).

Apostrophes

There are three uses for the apostrophe. The first is to indicate the possessive. The apostrophe comes before the final *s* if the word is singular (as in 'it was Management's decision') but it comes after the final *s* if the word is plural (as in 'it was the workers' decision' – i.e. *all* the workers, not just one of them). When the plural of a word is formed other than by adding an *s* the apostrophe comes before the final *s* (as in 'men's'). When the singular ends in *s* an additional *s* is written after the apostrophe if it is pronounced, but not if it is not pronounced. For example, 'St James's' is correct in the case of 'St James's Square' because 'James's' has two syllables but in other instances 'James'' might not be wrong.

The second use of the apostrophe is to indicate, in a contraction, that one or more letters have been omitted. Thus 'can't' means 'cannot', 'don't' means 'do not', etc. Note that 'it's' means 'it is' and not the possessive of 'it' which is 'its'. Contractions of the 'can't' and 'don't' variety and, indeed, all colloquialisms are best avoided in a business report. The language should be simple but not chatty.

The third use of the apostrophe is in phrases such as 'the 1920's' and the 'three R's', although it is also correct to write 'the 1920s' and 'the three Rs'.

Capitals

An initial capital letter in English is used for proper names or titles and also for adjectives such as 'English' which are derived from proper names. Confusion may arise where the same word has two different meanings depending on whether it starts with a capital letter or not. Thus 'production control' is the function carried out by the 'Production Control Department' which may be referred to as 'Production Control', omitting the 'Department'. Similarly 'management' is the function carried out by 'Management' where the latter is the collective term used to mean all managers or any manager in an organisation. 'The North' is a region whereas 'the north' is a direction.

Acronyms, words formed from the initial letters of other words, are often spelt out in capitals without full stops. Examples are: SHAPE, UNESCO, NATO, etc. Similarly, where firms are known by their initials alone the full stops are normally omitted, thus: IBM, ICI, ITT, C & A, etc. The practice of leaving out the full stops after initials has now been extended, as mentioned earlier, to all initial letters and abbreviations of names, titles, degrees, etc. Consider how ugly a list like 'I.B.M., I.C.I., I.T.T., C. and A.' would look. It is nevertheless advisable to keep the full stops in lower case abbreviations such as 'e.g.' and 'i.e.' in order to differentiate them from the surrounding words of the text. Also, there could be ambiguity in certain cases such as 'c.f.' (carried forward) and 'cf.' (confer, meaning compare with).

Italics

In the writing of business reports it is not generally practicable to use italics because of the limitations of the typewriters available. Using a machine with a 'golfball' or 'daisy wheel' it is theoretically possible to switch from one typeface to another and then back again. But this requires a great deal of time and effort on the part of the typist. Fortunately there are two practical alternatives. One is to underline the word which should be italicised. This is the device used to instruct a printer that a word *should* be in italics. The other alternative is to use quotation marks.

Italics are used for two purposes. One is to isolate a word or phrase in order to emphasise it – to make sure that however inattentive the reader may be his eye will be drawn to the italicised word and its significance will sink in. The other purpose is to indicate that it is the word itself rather than its meaning to which the reader's attention is being drawn. This need may arise when a familiar word is being used in an unfamiliar way or where for some particular reason it is necessary to use a foreign word or a dialect word. As a general rule, underline any words which ought to be italicised but bear in mind that it may occasionally be appropriate to use quotation marks where, ideally, one would choose italics.

Numbers

Words should be used for numbers up to a hundred unless there is a series of numbers, in which case numerals should be used. Numbers over one hundred should be written in numerals, except for round figures (hundreds, thousands, millions) which should be spelt out. Always use numerals for dates, telephone numbers, precise sums of money and exact measurements of all kinds. Write 'about ten feet' but write '10ft 2ins'.

The reason for these rules is that low numbers are easily read and understood when spelt out, but high numbers are cumbersome to write out in words, and are more easily read as numerals. Sums of money and dates are sometimes written out in full (e.g. on cheques or in wills) to make fraudulent alterations more difficult and also to ensure that a badly written figure is not misread. Such considerations do not normally apply to a typewritten business report.

Fractions such as a half, a quarter, two-thirds, etc., should be written out in words but more complicated fractions such as 22/7 or $1/\sqrt{2}$ should be written out using figures and the appropriate mathematical symbols.

Decimal fractions should always be expressed in figures. Write π ≃ 3.1416 and not 'pi is approximately equal to three point one four one six'.

Most typewriters have a selection of frequently occurring fractions, viz. ½, ¼, ¾, ⅓, ⅔. These should be used if they are sufficient. If the text or a table of figures includes fractions which are not on the typewriter then it will be necessary to type all fractions like this: 1/2, 7/12, 19/20, etc.

Percentages should be dealt with in the same way as other numbers. If they occur infrequently in the text, write them out in full: 'thirty-three per cent'. If they occur frequently and if they include fractions or decimals, use figures. If the number is given in words then 'per cent' should also be in words but if the number is given in figures then either 'per cent' or the percentage sign (%) can follow.

Never start a sentence with a numeral. The reason for this rule appears to be logical, namely, that a sentence must start with a capital letter and you cannot capitalise a numeral.

Columns of figures should be written out so that the decimal points are all in line, underneath one another. All numbers in a column should be given to the same number of decimal places. As a general rule the simpler the number the better, since it is easier to understand. Quite frequently the apparent accuracy of a figure implies an ability to measure something far more precisely than is actually possible. Certainly a cake can be divided into seven equal slices but £100 cannot be divided equally among seven people. You could give each person £14.28 but there would still be a fourpence left over. And £14.285714 has no real meaning.

Abbreviations

Where a number is written out in full the unit of measurement should also be written out in full. Where the number is given in figures the unit of measurement may also be abbreviated or a symbol may be used. Very large numbers may be expressed in terms of powers of ten (assuming that the readership is familiar with this notation). For example, 'twenty-five billion' may be written '25 × 10^9'. This incidentally clears up the possibility of ambiguity concerning the meaning of 'billion'. In most scientific circles and certainly in America a billion means a thousand times a million; some people still stick to the earlier definition of a million times a million.

Symbols should be used even more sparingly than abbreviations. Many symbols are not available on ordinary typewriters. Therefore, unless the complete set which you want is available, you will have to make do with words or abbreviations. For example, 'degrees', 'minutes' and 'seconds' can be abbreviated to 'degs.', 'mins.', and 'secs.', or symbols °, ′, ″, may be used. The symbol £ is particularly useful because the word 'pound' has two meanings. Symbols are useful in tabulations because the words for which the symbols stand might take up too much space in column headings.

There are some abbreviations which are almost invariably used and which require no explanation. These are styles of address, degrees and decorations. If there is any doubt write them out in full the first time and thereafter use the abbreviated form. In some cases the abbreviation is normal and the full word would sound or look strange. 'Mrs', which is short for 'mistress', is the obvious example of this.

6

Materials and equipment

The appearance of a report is perhaps not quite so important as the content. It is nevertheless very important. First impressions count and the reason why a report should be neatly typed and attractively bound is approximately the same as the reason why a person going for an interview should be neatly dressed and well groomed. The appearance of a report has a good or a bad effect on the reader before he has even begun to read it. The first part of a report to be seen is its cover.

Covers

It may be argued that in the case of a short report, say, up to half a dozen pages, no special covers are needed at all. For a fairly routine report written for internal circulation by an author who is already known, special covers are not needed. However, even if no covers are provided, it is still advisable to provide a title page (as already discussed in Chapter 2). This title page then effectively becomes the cover although it is printed on ordinary paper and stapled in the top left-hand corner. The title should be centred between a quarter and a third of the way down the page, in approximately the same place as the 'window' in a report cover. The remaining information (organisation, address, reference number, etc.), should appear at the foot of the page.

If the report is going outside the organisation or to a higher authority within the organisation, then it is advisable to put it inside covers, even if it is only half a dozen pages long. The primary purpose of covers is to protect the contents from becoming creased, stained or dog-eared. Covers also serve a number of secondary purposes. They are a form of packaging and as such they help to present the product (the report) to the consumer (the reader). The cover should make the report easy to identify among a heap of papers on a desk top or on a shelf. The cover also helps to project the 'image' of the author and of the organisation he works for. Finally the report cover may have to serve not only as a binding for the report itself but also for other relevant papers such as the minutes of a meeting held to discuss the contents of the report.

The simplest form of a report cover is a piece of card or art board cut to the same size or very slightly bigger than the paper (normally A4) on which the report is printed. A window cut in the front cover saves the preparation of labels or the printing of special covers for each report. Even if windows are cut in the front cover it is still a good idea to have the name of the organisation or a logo printed on the cover.

As regards the actual material there is some choice of colour and of finish but cost may be a constraining factor. Glossy, multi-coloured, printed covers are the most expensive; plain board, unprinted, ex-stock is the least expensive. As an alternative to board there are various types of plastic and imitation leather covers. The use of a transparent cover can also be effective, depending on the quality of the printing on the sheet which is underneath it.

Colours, as psychologists know, can be highly significant and can either be a help or a hindrance in giving the impression which the writer wants to give. Different shades have different meanings and there may be special associations between a particular colour and the products of an organisation, e.g. black and coal, grey and steel, cream and dairy products. In general:

- Green and blue are 'safe' colours, normally associated with the sea, the sky and the countryside.

- Grey and beige are neutral colours, quiet and un-obtrusive.

- Yellow and orange are 'happy' colours, sunny and warm. They are also somewhat ostentatious, to be used if you want to draw attention to yourself.

- Red is a 'dangerous' colour, the colour of blood, fire, violence and passion. Purple has similar overtones.

- Pink and mauve are 'gentle' colours, soft and feminine.

- Brown is a 'dirty' colour, the colour of earth and of excrement. In certain contexts brown can also be a 'warm' colour, the colour of coffee, tea, bread, eggs, etc. Much depends on the precise shade.

- Black signifies darkness, satanic forces, gloom and doom.

- White represents cleanliness and purity but is not recommended for report covers because it merges with all the other papers on a person's desk and in any case it gets dirty too easily.

Combinations of colours can be used and, to some extent,

colours used in combination have an effect which is different from that of the same colours used separately. Thus black by itself is funereal but combined with yellow, silver or gold the effect is entirely different. Similarly red, white and blue (at least in Britain, France, the USA and some other countries), have patriotic significance.

The cover of a report must be considered together with the method of binding since the latter also has an important effect on the general appearance of the document.

Binding

There are several ways in which a report may be bound. Perhaps the most popular is the method known as 'comb binding'. Reports to be bound by this method are punched using a special machine which puts a row of rectangular perforations down the left-hand side of the page. A plastic spine with numerous little teeth is fitted into the punched holes. In order to do this the spine has to be held open using a special jig. Without this device it is almost impossible to take out or insert pages without tearing them. The spines should be the correct size for the thickness of paper being bound, otherwise the appearance will be marred. Various colours are available to match or to contrast with the colour of the report cover. The machine used for binding can also be used for 'unbinding' so that extra sheets can be inserted if necessary.

An alternative method of binding uses wire in a very similar way. Both these methods have the advantage that the report can be opened out flat. Methods which effectively squeeze or clip the pages together are less satisfactory from the point of view of reading the report: the pages have to be creased or held open. Reports which are clipped together or in which the pages are stuck together by a heat-sealing process in the manner of a paperback book also have the disadvantage that there is no proper spine to the document. Therefore, when placed on a shelf it has no means of identification. Very few types of binding permit an identification to be given on the spine. This difficulty particularly applies to thin reports: thick reports can usually be marked in some way even if not very elegantly. Reports are often kept together with other papers in filing cabinets or box files where identification on the spine serves no purpose. The ideal method of report binding, provided that cost is not a primary consideration, would appear to be a form of ring binder. The most commonly used ring binder is much too thick for the average report, but a range of small sizes should be available. Fifty pages is a fair sized report but still amounts to no more than a quarter of an inch thickness of paper. The popular ring binder also has only two rings, for which holes can be made with the kind of punch which is available from most stationers. The ideal binder for a report would have at least four and possibly six or eight rings and this implies the need for a special punch. If there are only two rings there is a danger that pages will become detached. Other features of the ideal report cover/binder include:

- a pocket, so that other relevant documents can be kept in the same folder (rather than attached with a paper clip);

- a window or label holder, so that the report title can be seen without the need to open the document;

- a label holder or other means of identification on the spine, so that the report can be identified on a shelf;

- the organisation's name and/or logo printed on the front cover.

Different types of binding are illustrated in Figure 6.1.

If you cannot buy exactly what you want for your particular report it will certainly be worthwhile to have covers made specially. Give your report covers the same kind of attention which is given to sales literature, brochures and so on. Make sure that the most important recipients of a report are given elegantly bound copies even if, in the interests of economy, other people have to make do with more cheaply bound copies.

Photoreduction

A method which is sometimes used effectively to produce fairly short reports and research papers inexpensively is photoreduction. Use A3 (for paper sizes, see p. 90) and type two A4-sized pages on each sheet; then photo-reduce to A4 size. (Instead of using A3 paper, the manuscript can be prepared in the normal way on A4 paper and two sheets placed side by side on the copying machine.) The pages can then be stapled in the middle, using a long-armed stapler, to make an A5-sized booklet. If the paper is printed on both sides, four folded A4 sheets make a sixteen-page booklet. The saving on paper leaves more money to spend on attractive printed covers. Alternatively, an A4-sized report can be produced using A3 sheets, folded, stapled and trimmed if necessary. This is certainly preferable to clipping A4 sheets down the edge so that they will not open properly.

Paper

The 'substance' of paper is measured in grammes per square metre (gsm). The paper normally used for duplicating reports has a substance of 80 gsm. For a more impressive appearance a paper of heavier substance (90 gsm) may be used. (For comparison purposes the paper

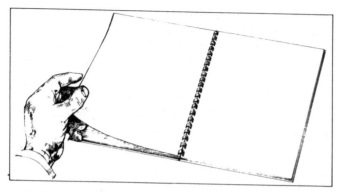

a) Plastic comb binder

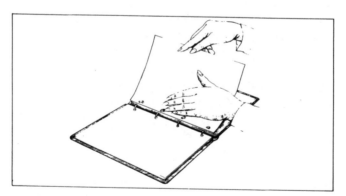

b) Four ring binder

Figure 6.1
Types of binding

used for normal typing is a 70 gsm 'bond' paper and the flimsy copies are a 45 gsm 'bank' paper).

Some organisations like to use paper on which their name or logo appears either in the top right-hand corner or at the foot of the page. This may be seen as advertising or 'image projection' but it is no protection against unauthorised copying. The best place for the name or logo is on the cover and/or the title page. To repeat it on every subsequent page could be said to be overdoing it.

Coloured paper may sometimes be used to good effect. For example, the summary section or the appendices might be distinguished from the main body of the report by being printed on paper of a different shade. Use only pale-tinted paper and use only one additional colour per report. If every chapter is a different colour the effect is unattractive. If dark colours are used there is a danger that the reader will have difficulty in reading the print.

Note on paper sizes

It should perhaps be explained that in the series of 'Continental' paper sizes: A0, A1, A2, A3, A4, A5, etc., each size is half the size of the previous one and *exactly the same shape*. Thus when an A4 sheet is cut in half (down the middle of the long side) two A5 sheets result, the ratio of the short to the long sides remaining the same, i.e. as one is to the square root of two (1:1.4142). The actual A4 size is 21.0 x 29.7 centimetres but it is the shape which has the unique property. This feature of the A0 series has important implications for printing and photoreduction. It will be readily appreciated that a sheet of foolscap (in which the ratio of short to long sides is 1:1.625) if folded in two would produce a very different shape (in which the ratio of short to long sides is 1:1.2308). In other words a foolscap sheet would have to be reduced to a quarter of its size (by cutting in both dimensions) in order to give the same shape again. The same applies to the quarto and the brief sizes which have now been to a large extent superseded by A4 and A3. A reduction to a quarter of the original size is not generally practicable and any other reduction, except of a sheet having the magic $1/\sqrt{2}$ formula, will yield peculiar margins. It is also generally agreed that the rectangle in which the ratio of the sides is $1/\sqrt{2}$ is an aesthetically pleasing shape.

Typefaces

A variety of typefaces is now available and any manufacturer or supplier of typewriters or word processing equipment will provide a card or booklet containing examples of the range which he offers. Three character spacing alternatives are usually available: 10 pitch (i.e. ten characters to the inch), 12 pitch and proportional spacing. In the old days, before the invention of the golfball typewriter or of proportional spacing there was little choice other than 'Elite' (12 pitch) and 'Pica' (10 pitch). Nowadays it is easy to change from one typeface to another and numerous styles are available including gothic and italic styles as well as those more usually associated with the typewriter. Some examples are given in Figure 6.2.

It is necessary to decide which styles are to be used for what purposes. Many people think that proportional spacing looks best. This allows different widths for different letters as illustrated in Figure 6.3.

However, using an ordinary typewriter, corrections are easier without proportional spacing and typists generally prefer 12 pitch. This is more economical than 10 pitch, giving 20 per cent more words in the same space. It also permits more columns in a table of figures and gives fewer

PICA 10

Xerox print wheels are available in a wide
range of type styles and three character
spacing alternatives: 10 pitch, 12 pitch,
and Proportional Spacing, so there is a
style to suit every application. All print
wheels are metal coated for durability
and, used with a ribbon from the Xerox
range, will produce high quality text.

+*"/@£_&'()?¡QWERTYUIOP#¼ASDFGHJKL:¢ZXCVBNM,.%

=1234567890-½qwertyuiop!⅜asdfghjkl;$zxcvbnm,.½

SCIENTIFIC 10 +•·}≡;_∑^(){ΠΓΔ÷Θ™Ξ}↑ℓ←.∇ΣΦ<Λ¶∫§Ω°{≈∞Ψ∝|∽∂`···±

₀1234567890 _:γδεΘτυξ↓↑ρ∕,ασφ>λη∫κω→ζχψ†βυμˉ˜π

Figure 6.2
Type styles. A small selection of many available styles is illustrated. Reproduced by kind permission of Rank
Xerox (UK) Limited.

ELITE 12

Xerox print wheels are available in a wide range
of type styles and three character spacing alternatives:
10 pitch, 12 pitch, and Proportional Spacing,
so there is a style to suit every application.
All print wheels are metal coated for durability
and, used with a ribbon from the Xerox range, will
produce high quality text.

+*"/@£_&'()?¼QWERTYUIOP#⅓ASDFGHJKL:¢ZXCVBNM,.%

=1234567890-¾qwertyuiop!⅔asdfghjkl;$zxcvbnm,.½

**LETTER
GOTHIC 12**

Xerox print wheels are available in a wide range
of type styles and three character spacing alternatives:
10 pitch, 12 pitch, and Proportional Spacing,
so there is a style to suit every application.
All print wheels are metal coated for durability
and, used with a ribbon from the Xerox range, will
produce high quality text.

+*"/@£_&'()?¼QWERTYUIOP#⅓ASDFGHJKL:¢ZXCVBNM,.%

=1234567890-¾qwertyuiop!⅔asdfghjkl;$zxcvbnm,.½

Figure 6.2 (continued)

BOLD ITALIC

Xerox print wheels are available in a wide range of type styles and three character spacing alternatives: 10 pitch, 12 pitch, and Proportional Spacing, so there is a style to suit every application. All print wheels are metal coated for durability and, used with a ribbon from the Xerox range, will produce high quality text.

+*"/@£_&'()?¼QWERTYUIOP[]ASDFGHJKL;²ZXCVBNM,.%°>

=1234567890-¾qwertyuiop!³asdfghjkl;$zxcvbnm,.½μ<

GOTHIC

Xerox print wheels are available in a wide range of type styles and three character spacing alternatives: 10 pitch, 12 pitch, and Proportional Spacing, so there is a style to suit every application. All print wheels are metal coated for durability and, used with a ribbon from the Xerox range, will produce high quality text.

+*"/@£_&'()?¼QWERTYUIOP#⅓ASDFGHJKL;¢ZXCVBNM,.%

=1234567890-¾qwertyuiop!⅔asdfghjkl;$zxcvbnm,.½

Figure 6.2 (concluded)

abcdefghijklmnopqrstuvwxyz

ABCDEFGHIJKLMNOPQRSTUVWXYZ

1234567890

iiiiiiiiii
kkkkkkkkkk
wwwwwwwwww
mmmmmmmmmm

Figure 6.3
Proportional spacing (IBM 'Executive'). In practice letters average out at twelve to the inch as in the word 'organisation'.

problems with hyphenation. Proportional spacing is almost the same from a space point of view, as 12 pitch since on most machines most of the letters in proportional spacing are 12 pitch. Most of the capitals are wider than 12 pitch; lower case f, i, j, l and t are narrower than 12 pitch, w and m are wider. Figures are of course all the same (12 pitch) otherwise there would be difficulty with tabular material.

It is best to decide on one particular typeface for normal use in reports. If several different typefaces are used it will be counterproductive to the organisation's aim of presenting a consistent image. Occasionally it may be desirable to use two different typefaces within a report, for example, using italics for the summary or for quotations. It is also highly desirable that the 'scientific' typeface should be available for use when appropriate. This has the Greek letters, mathematical symbols and small figures for use as subscripts and superscripts. All these look very messy if they have to be improvised or written in by hand.

Reprographic methods

The three methods most readily available nowadays for the reproduction of reports are: the automatic typewriter or word processor which produces 'top copies' – these are described below; the copying machine which uses the xerographic or heat fusion process and which is used for small runs or runs of medium length; and the small offset press which is used to produce long runs of high quality. Other methods such as the use of carbon copies, the ink duplicator and the hectographic (spirit) duplicator are less satisfactory and have generally been superseded by the first three methods mentioned. Coloured carbon ribbons are available for use with word processors but, of course, copiers normally work only with black. If multicoloured diagrams, charts, maps, etc., are required it is best to go to a commercial printer although small amounts of colour can be added by hand.

Office copiers come in a variety of styles and sizes. The more expensive models are not only faster but have facilities for reduction and can be coupled up to a collator. Reduction facilities are particularly useful when it is necessary to reproduce a table or chart the original of which has had to be typed or drawn on a sheet which is larger than the standard size required. The collator can be used to produce batches of, in most cases, up to twenty copies of a report.

It is essential that the copier should be properly maintained and serviced, otherwise quality will suffer and breakdowns are more likely to occur. If the process of copying is interrupted for any reason the chances are greatly increased that a mistake will be made. Having spent much time and effort on the report it would be most annoying to be late because of a breakdown of the copier or to have recipients complain that pages are upside down or missing or in the wrong order. It is therefore very important that when the report is finally bound it is also checked. The fact that pages have been numbered is of great help in this checking process. If the pages are not numbered one must look at the actual words to ensure that the pages are in the right order and that none are missing.

Word processors

A word processing system consists essentially of a small computer with a screen, for editing text, and a printer. The versatility of the system depends on the nature of the software and on the type of printer.

A basic word processing system such as 'Wordstar' functions like a typewriter but more efficiently and with certain additional facilities.

- Text can be centred, justified or unjustified.
- Text can be inserted, deleted or moved.
- Margins and tab stops can be set.
- Pages can be numbered.
- Headings can be repeated automatically on each page.
- Spacing can be single, double or triple.

Some word processing packages incorporate a 'spellchecker', a dictionary of some 80,000 words, which is useful for correcting genuine spelling mistakes and also for spotting typing errors, for example, where letters are inadvertently transposed.

Depending on the kind of printer used, various type styles are available with 10, 12 or 15 characters to the inch. The 'daisy-wheel' printer produces 'letter quality' text, while the 'dot matrix' printer offers 'near letter quality' (NLQ) text or 'draft' text at a faster speed. Simple charts and graphs can also be produced using the 'dot matrix' printer. 'Inkjet' and 'laser' printers are more versatile and can be used, in conjunction with graphics packages, to produce complex flow charts and text with several different fonts. For coloured diagrams, maps and other complex shapes the use of a plotter is indicated.

'Integrated software' usually refers to linked programs for word processing, databases (typically used for updating and rearranging complex lists and catalogues) and spreadsheets (used for accounting purposes and various calculations). 'Lotus 1-2-3' and derivatives, 'Smart' and 'Appleworks' are well known systems. Database files and spreadsheet files can be 'imported' into the word processor files and incorporated into the final document, with the appropriate headings and pages correctly numbered.

From integrated software and graphics packages it is a small step to 'desktop publishing' pioneered by Apple Computer Inc. A desktop publishing system enables one to produce documents which are almost indistinguishable from those provided by the professional printer. Pages are made up on screen with illustrations shrunk to whatever size is required to fit in with the text. Illustrations can be 'read' by a scanner and copied directly onto the screen. Printing is by laser printer. A report produced by this method is very much superior in appearance to one which has been cobbled together by a combination of typing, drawing, cutting and pasting, which until quite recently has been the accepted approach.

The next development is an inexpensive colour reprographic system, used for making copies in full colour of maps and diagrams from plotters or from original artwork.

Electronic filing systems

An important feature of word processing systems is their facility for providing compact and secure filing of information. If it is necessary to keep a copy of every report produced in an organisation in some central location then the sheer volume of these copies may present a problem. If the same information is held on disks one filing cabinet can be used to store the same amount of material as twenty cabinets full of printed material. The same claim could be made for microfilm systems, but information kept on disks is more secure because the risk of unauthorised use is minimal. This is a great advantage when dealing with highly confidential reports which may be stolen or copied by unauthorised persons.

However, a floppy disk containing the text of a report can be protected in a number of ways which are not possible in the case of written or printed matter. In the first place the disk need not be identified other than by a code number. If the disk is loaded on to the machine it can be protected by another password which the operator would need to know before any text appeared on the screen. Additional coded instructions could prevent anyone from either printing or altering the text without knowing the relevant passwords.

Charts and diagrams

Charts and diagrams can make or mar a report. Some comments have already been made in Chapter 2. If the author of a report has no talent as a draughtsman or graphic designer, he would be wise to seek professional advice. However, there are a number of aids available which the amateur can use to give a professional appearance to his work.

Various templates, stencils and French curves are available for the drawing of boxes, symbols and lines on graphs. In addition, dry print is available for the reproduction of letters, figures and symbols which cannot be typed. The use of dry print can be particularly effective for title pages and chapter headings. It is also useful for shading such as may be required in the preparation of plans and certain types of chart.

Graph paper often does not reproduce well on a copying machine and it is sometimes preferable to trace a graph on to plain paper before copying.

7

Planning

The writing of a report is not just something which can be tacked on to the end of a project or investigation. On the contrary, the report is always an essential part of the job. Sometimes the presentation of information in the form of a report is actually the main objective. It is therefore vital to consider the report from the outset, to plan the various stages in the preparation of the report as part of the plan for the whole task. This means thinking of the report in terms of the job. The two should be inseparable. If you have done work which is not going to be mentioned in the report (because it is irrelevant) then ask yourself why you did it. If there are things which need to be said in the report and you have not had time to do the necessary work, this also suggests bad planning.

It is necessary at the beginning of the exercise to be very clear in your mind that you understand the questions which the client wants to be answered. Then, as work proceeds, ask yourself all the time: is this relevant? Does this help to answer the question? Is there anything else which needs to be investigated?

Check your findings as you go along. Keep your client informed. Have progress meetings. Give an oral presentation of results at the end of the project, before the final report is issued. This will give an opportunity to test reactions and make any last minute changes. It will also alert the client so that he is not surprised by the contents of the report when he eventually reads it. He will then be more likely to accept it. As a final safeguard, submit a couple of copies of your report a few days early with the word 'DRAFT' stamped on them. This will give the client an opportunity to spot any unfortunate words or phrases, and give you time to correct them, before any damage is done. With a little luck there will be no changes to make – but it is far better to rely on checking and double-checking everything than to rely on luck.

The schedule

The essence of the planning process is the division of a piece of work into stages and the allocation of the necessary time and resources to each stage. An attempt is then made to stick to the timetable which has been set and progress is monitored as work proceeds. If you fall behindhand then the rest of the job will have to be replanned. You will eat into your contingency allowance and you may have to ask for an extension. There is always a great danger that the two weeks, say, which were allowed for report writing, become one week and the one week becomes three days. You will then find yourself writing all through the weekend, hoping to catch the post on Monday when the report should have been delivered the previous Friday. This is a recipe for disaster: a hurriedly written report delivered late.

The writing of a report should be planned with meticulous care. The necessary time should be allocated to the report and not diverted to other purposes. One of the best ways to prevent this diversion of time is to set a deadline for the 'end' of the practical work, calling this, if you like, the 'end' of the project. Then agree that the report will be delivered two weeks from that date. If for any reason the 'end' of the project slips, the deadline for the report will slip with it. You really do need time to finalise the report after all the other work has finished. If essential information is still trickling in while you are writing down your conclusions there is a distinct possibility that those conclusions may be wrong.

The skeleton report

One of the first things to be done at the beginning of an exercise is to draw up a 'skeleton report'. This is a list of the main chapter headings and a list of the subjects to be covered under each heading. Relate the skeleton report to the terms of reference. Make quite sure that your plan covers all the terms of reference and does not include extraneous material which, however interesting, was not actually requested. If you feel strongly, after having started the work, that there is something wrong with the terms of reference, then see if you can get them changed by mutual agreement.

Assembling the raw material

As you proceed, step by step, to execute your plan of work (collecting information, conducting experiments, interviewing people) you will also be collecting material for the report. All your notes, calculations, graphs, letters written and received, papers you have read, are potentially useful for the report. Take rough notes as you go along and write up those notes carefully later in the day. If you leave this chore for twenty-four hours you will find that you have forgotten important facts. It is very difficult to write a convincing report based on incomplete and scruffy notes. However, well written notes, accumulated over a period can often be incorporated, with a little editing, into the text of the report. This can speed up the production of the report without jeopardising its quality. Writing can be mentally exhausting and there is a limit to the amount of work which can be satisfactorily accomplished in a given time. Many professional writers discipline themselves to produce two thousand words a day. Reports, like most other things in this world, require 10 per cent talent and 90 per cent hard work. You cannot expect to be inspired. In general it is wise to allow at least a week for the production of a ten thousand word report.

Drafting

It is normal for a report to go through at least one draft before a final version is produced. One draft should be enough but if extensive alterations have to be made for some reason or other, then a second draft may be needed so that alterations to the alterations can be made. Third drafts are not unknown, particularly where a report is produced by a committee. However, there comes a point when one must call a halt. If the meaning is still not clear and if there are still errors of fact after three attempts, then there is probably something wrong with the person producing the report. What is more likely to happen is that time runs out so that the report has to be issued in any case, even though it leaves something to be desired.

It is not easy to get complex ideas down on paper. The problem can be tackled in two stages. First the content: write it down as it comes and never mind the form. Then the form: rewrite it paying particular attention to grammar and syntax and clarity of style. If the meaning is still not clear perhaps this is because a step in the logic has been omitted. An extra sentence or a parenthesis needs to be inserted. These alterations should be made by the author on his manuscript before he passes it on to the typist.

Some writers prefer to send the first, hastily scribbled, 'as it comes' version away for typing and then make extensive alterations to the typed draft. This is a costly and time-consuming procedure, especially if the manuscript is untidy and partly illegible. (Typing pools in some organisations have strict rules about the quality of the manuscripts that they will accept.) Bad handwriting should not be allowed to impede the production of a report. A writer who cannot write fast enough to keep up with his thoughts and maintain legibility could perhaps adopt the 'notetaking' technique: jotting down the key words or phrases and constructing the sentences later. Another solution might be to learn shorthand, or to use a tape recorder.

There are some dangers in the use of dictation as a means for producing a report. The spoken word is not the same as the written word. The meaning of the words on the tape can be perfectly clear to the listener but, when transcribed, appear ambiguous. Natural speech is not easily punctuated. To produce a satisfactory text from a tape often involves a total rewrite. So, in the end, time will have been wasted rather than saved. The tape recorder can, however, be used by an author who speaks from extensive notes. He must get the paragraph numbers right and pay attention to punctuation. Some audio typists are able to infer from the inflection of the voice where the commas and full stops should go. However, semicolons and colons should be dictated, proper names should be spelt out, brackets and quotation marks should be given. The secret of effective dictation is to make sure the sentences are short and simple. But remember that good style demands that some sentences should be longer than others. Otherwise the prose will seem staccato and 'action packed' like the description of a fight in an Ian Fleming novel. It is quite possible to spend *longer* on dictation (including playbacks, erasures and long pauses for thought), than would have been spent writing the text out, reading it through and making changes to the manuscript.

Timing

At forty words a minute (which is not particularly fast for a typist) a ten thousand-word report should take just over four hours to produce. In practice two days is more like the time which should be allowed. This is because typing a report is not a straight copy-typing job. Time has to be allowed for checking, correcting, preparation of tabular material, numbering of pages, discussing layout problems and, of course, natural breaks.

The time required to duplicate, collate, punch and bind twenty copies of a ten thousand-word report is also about four hours. Once again it would be wise to allow some time for contingencies. In other words, if the final script is not available for typing to start on the Wednesday morning, it is quite likely that the report will not be available for despatch on the Friday. However, if it is intended that the client or a colleague should see a 'draft' copy of the report and that any comments should be taken on board before the final version is produced, then another two days should be allowed. Therefore, an author should aim to have the final draft of his report available for typing on the Monday if he is to meet a Friday deadline having carried out all the desirable checks.

These considerations, plus the fact that the writer cannot be expected to produce the manuscript at a rate much faster than two thousand words a day leads to the conclusion that one should allow a fortnight after the 'end' of a project to produce the report. A long report might well be produced in the same time with more people working on it; a short report could be produced in less time, but it is very unwise to try to hurry the production of any significant document. Even a short document, which could be written and typed in a day, should preferably not be issued on that same day. The author should draft it on one day, sleep on it, read it again the next day, pencil in any suggested improvements, get a colleague to read it through and make comments, then have it retyped.

A methodical approach such as has been described is important if a report is to do credit to the author and to the organisation which he represents. If not enough time is allowed, or if deadlines are brought forward, then staff will be working under undesirable pressure and it is in these conditions that mistakes are made. Work very hard by all means but always leave enough time to check the work that has been done and to rectify any errors which may be detected.

Editorial control

All reports require editing to some extent. The author of a short report will normally edit his own work but should also ask a colleague to look through it and make constructive comments. In the case of reports where two or more authors are involved the editorial task is more difficult – and more important. One person must assume overall responsibility for the report even though he may write only a small part of it himself. He would have to write the summary of the report even if the main sections were written by other people. The task of the report editor is that of project controller where the 'project' is the production of the report. He is not necessarily the person in charge of the investigation as a whole, although he might well be. A significant report produced for a government department normally has a report secretary. In other situations the same duties might be performed by a project co-ordinator or by the personal assistant to the project director. The essential points to be covered are:

Skeleton report: Ensure that a skeleton report is drawn up at an early stage and that the various parts of the report are allocated to the appropriate members of the team. Each person will then know exactly what subjects are to be his responsibility; nothing will be omitted and nothing duplicated.

Schedule: Agree with each author a date by which his section of the report is to be submitted in draft form. This is necessary since it will not be possible to put the whole report together or to summarise it until all the individual sections have been received.

'Signing off': Ascertain that each author has checked and double-checked his facts, particularly where these may be controversial. Perhaps the worst thing which anyone can do in a report is to draw an astonishing conclusion from facts which are assumed to be correct but which are actually erroneous. Try to develop the faculty for spotting errors – not just linguistic lapses but, more importantly, arithmetic mistakes and faulty reasoning. Take a leaf out of the television interviewer's book and say to the contributor: 'Let me see if I have correctly understood what you are saying...' and then repeat back the argument using different words and drawing attention to any implications which may not have been immediately obvious. Remember: you are unlikely to spot errors unless you understand the material you are editing. And if you do not understand it, who will? How can you write a summary of it or explain it to a third party?

Consistency: The style of the report must be consistent from chapter to chapter even when each chapter has been written by a different person. When the drafts are submitted one may be excellent, another pompous and full of padding, another chatty and full of colloquialisms. Extensive rewriting may be necessary. It may well happen that the good ones are on time and the bad ones, which require most attention, are late. A person who keeps letting the side down because of the poor quality and/or lateness of his written work must either get better or get out. You cannot go on carrying him for ever.

It is difficult but not impossible to improve somebody's language skills, but do not expect miracles from sending staff on a one-day course in report writing! This may be a very good beginning but it will need constant reinforcement. More practice plus the occasional discipline of having to check through and edit other people's work should lead to significant improvement in the long run.

Office services: Make sure that the administrative staff are warned of the date when the manuscript is expected to be available for typing; let them know the approximate length of the report and whether there are likely to be any particular difficulties with tabular material, illustrations, fold-out sections and so on. Discuss problems with the relevant staff and be sympathetic. Remember that other reports and documents are also scheduled to be produced by the same office staff and, if yours is late, there is a danger that other reports may be late also. Alternatively, the cost of 'catching up' may be high; it may be necessary to work overtime or take on extra temporary staff to cope with the backlog.

And finally ... Keep a note of all the people to whom copies of the report are sent; keep a copy for yourself; see that there is a copy in the departmental file and that the masters are retained in case further copies have to be run off. (Taking a copy of a copy is not always a satisfactory procedure.) If there is a sudden urgent need for another copy, the departmental copy can be released and replaced later.

It is also a very good idea to prepare an abstract or a one-page summary of the report at this stage, while the exercise is fresh in your mind. An annual report containing well-written summaries of all the reports produced by your organisation during the year can be a most impressive document – and very simple to produce if the summaries are already written.

Exercises

The reader is invited to analyse the following passages which contain examples of bad English, and suggest improvements; this author's comments follow each extract.

The first extract is taken from an actual proposal for consultancy work in the field of marketing. It is an example of the kind of writing which, unfortunately, is often found today. There are numerous examples of words wrongly used and a dozen other types of error. The sentences are numbered for reference in the commentary which follows. The names are fictitious.

(1) Following the recent appraisal undertaken by XYZ, the management has accepted the need for implementing greater Group integration within the Bloggs companies. (2) In order for the Group to present a common image it must show a consistent level of performance across all operating units particularly in terms of marketing and sales skills. (3) To obtain this the Board has accepted that central management must play a greater part in directing each company's activities, although it is recognised that the autonomy of each company must be retained. (4) It is also

accepted that significant sales increases can be
achieved in the short term by improving the overall
Group standard of sales management and control ... (5)
The sales control system should take into account the
need for simplicity thereby maximising real selling
time ... (6) The role of individual sales management
will be to evaluate their respective sales operations,
constantly and critically ... (7) From this study the
most appropriate system will be selected and then
adapted to incorporate the specific operational
characteristics of the Bloggs Group. (8) As the system
evolves, it will be corroborated by reference back to the
individual companies in order to ensure comparability
with national requirements.

Comment

(1) 'appraisal' of what?
'management' of what? Or should it be 'Management'
with a capital M?
'accepted the need': surely not! Recognised, perhaps.
'implementing': either leave this word out or expand
the phrase to 'implementing the XYZ recommendation that ...'
'greater Group integration': this is not what is meant.
The individual companies may be integrated, if that is
what was meant, not the Group. However, integration
means loss of identity. Perhaps 'co-operation' or even
'standardisation of procedures' was intended.

(2) 'In order for ... to' is clumsy and not standard
English. 'common image': the group, being singular,
can have only one image. The individual companies
could present a common image, i.e. all have the same
image.

'consistent level': the same applies – consistent with what? The levels (plural) of the individual operating units could be the same.

'performance' of what?

'in terms of': one does not perform in terms, one performs in the thing itself, i.e. in marketing. One does not perform in a skill, one has or develops or acquires a skill.

The whole sentence would have been clearer if 'operating units' had been made the subject and the more usual order used of subject/verb/object/dependent clause.

(3) 'To obtain this': what? Consistency of level(s)?

'accepted': this time the meaning is 'agreed'.

'play a greater part in directing': i.e. 'direct more of'.

'although ...' The second part of the sentence contradicts the first. If some activities are directed by an outsider then some autonomy is lost. If this autonomy 'must be retained' then Central Management must play no part in directing. Perhaps what the writer meant to say was something like 'While it is desirable that the autonomy of each company should be retained as far as possible, there are some functions which must be directed from the centre.'

(4) 'accepted': this time the meaning is 'believed'.

'improving the overall Group standard': Ugh! Why not try something like 'a general improvement in ...'

(5) 'need for simplicity ...': this is a non-sequitur as well as being bad grammar. It should presumably read 'need to maximise selling time' (Whether a simple system will do this or not is not implicit in the need. A

sophisticated system might be more effective. It depends on what you mean.)

'real selling time': what else is selling time other than real? Fictitious? Imaginary?

(6) 'The role of individual sales management': presumably what was meant was 'each sales manager'. As it stands it is nonsense.

'evaluate': review would make more sense; or substitute 'performance' for 'operation'.

'constant': i.e. at regular intervals.

'critical': this would apply to 'review' or 'examination', not 'evaluation'.

(7) 'incorporate': i.e. 'take account of'.

'specific': i.e. 'particular'.

(8) 'corroborated': obviously the wrong word. The writer may have meant 'seen to be justified' or possibly 'need to be modified'.

'comparability': this looks as if it might be a typing error for 'compatibility'. Alternatively the writer may have meant 'to comply with national legislation'.

The second example is taken from a report recommending improvements to the production control system in an engineering factory. The prose is turgid, and pompous phrases are frequently used to disguise a very simple thought. The opening phrase is a classic example of this all too common fault. Read through the following paragraphs with a view to providing a simpler and clearer version.

Notwithstanding the present adverse trading

situation much can be done with existing resources and a very modest outlay of funds to improve productivity and reduce waste. The difficulties and problems may be no more than growing pains of an organisation which in two years has seen its labour force grown (*sic*) from around ten to the present level of fifty. Management and supervisory practices which were no doubt more than adequate two years ago are however unlikely to be appropriate given the present manufacturing methods. To put the situation in a better context, should the next two years see the same sort of growth and expansion as that occurring since 1978 then certainly the situation will become more complex and the need for more systematic management become even more critical.

Rightly, the XYZ report indicated serious short-comings in the functional areas of production planning and control, almost certainly resulting in under-utilisation of resources, low levels of efficiency and excess costs. While there was insufficient time available in this investigation to quantify those conditions there was sufficient evidence to hand to confirm considerable potential for improvement in manufacturing efficiency, work flow, supervision and individual productivity. The following items are a list of the more obvious courses (*sic*) of inefficiency, wasted time and effort, frustration and low output.

(a) bad housekeeping
(b) too much reliance on passing instructions verbally
(c) inadequate record keeping
(d) no proper checking procedures
(e) lack of suitable containers, bins and storage facilities

(f) ad hoc planning, progressing and co-ordination procedures

In essence all of these reduce to the basic and prime necessity of having the right materials available in the right place, in the right time, in the right quantity if manufacturing is to proceed smoothly and efficiently. Whilst appreciating that the above conditions are not helped while the factory is going through a relayout it is the considered opinion of the author that while the physical re-organisation can do a lot to help management overcome their difficulties, without additional support in the form of suitable operational and administrative procedures then the full possibilities for optimising production capacity will be missed.

Most of the features listed above can be tackled almost immediately and the following sections of this report describe techniques appropriate to the primary objective referred to above ...

Before an alternative version of this piece is given there are a few remarks to be made on this author's use of English. There is a general dearth of commas leading, in one case, to ambiguity. 'Low levels of efficiency and excess costs' implies excess costs at a low level when the context makes it clear that excess costs would be high. 'Grown' (line 6) should be 'grow'; 'courses (line 25) should be 'causes'. A frequent error is to use the word 'verbal' to mean 'oral' (as opposed to written). 'Verbal' of course means using words (as opposed to pictures or numbers). Sentences beginning 'Whilst appreciating' should have a person as the subject: an inanimate object or 'it' is incapable of appreciating in a transitive sense. Finally (last sentence) 'features' cannot be 'tackled' but problems can.

Alternative version

Although cash may be short, there is much that can be done at low cost and making use of existing resources, to improve productivity and reduce waste. The number of staff has been increased from ten to fifty in two years and some of the problems now being encountered are almost certainly due to 'growing pains'. Manufacturing methods have become more sophisticated which means that some of the original management and supervisory procedures are no longer adequate. If expansion continues at the same rate during the next two years then there is no doubt that changes in the methods and techniques of management and control will be urgently required.

The XYZ report indicated that there were deficiencies in the production planning and control system leading to inefficient use of resources and excess costs. While it had not been possible in the time available to quantify these inefficiencies, it was evident that there was ample scope for improvement in a number of areas such as work flow supervision, plant and labour productivity. The most obvious reasons for inefficiency were: (same list as previously quoted).

Efficiency in production depends very much on having the right materials in the right place at the right time. This necessary condition is unlikely to be satisfied until all the faults which have been listed are remedied. The layout of the factory has been replanned and alterations are in progress. This is causing some difficulty but, when complete, these changes will certainly be beneficial. At the same time there will be an opportunity to introduce new control procedures and make the best possible use of the production facilities. This opportunity should not be missed.

'There is no reason for delay in tackling these problems and the necessary steps are outlined in the remaining sections of this report . . .'

The third and fourth examples are concerned with the 'Fog Index'. If a piece of writing has a high Fog Index it means that the sentences are too long and that there are too many long words. The Fog Index was developed in America. It is calculated as follows:

(a) Count the number of words in each sentence in the passage to be analysed and work out the average.

(b) Add the percentage of words of more than two syllables.

The Fog Index: Example 1

There now follows the text of a bulletin issued in March 1977 by the Management of Leyland Cars. It has a Fog Index of 51. The average sentence is 35 words long and 16 out of every 100 words have three of more syllables. See if you can do better. When you have finished, compare your version with the version produced by journalists from The Sunday Times which is quoted immediately following the original.

For the attention of plant directors and equivalent and for communication to employees as appropriate.

Derek Whittaker has made it clear to all Plant Participation Committees in his recent visits that neither he nor his directors will be submitting any major capital expenditure for final approval to either the British Leyland Board or the National Enterprise

Board unless he has commitments to the necessary improvements in productivity from employees representatives of all sections and all management involved in the respective project.

After full discussion of the ADO 88 project at Leyland Cars Joint Management Committee and at the special sub-committee the council set up to study it, the programme was agreed. The council also agreed that the Programme be presented to the Joint Management Committees and senior representatives in the plants concerned to obtain their endorsement. Endorsement has been obtained from all plants except Longbridge where meetings are being held today at shop floor level seeking a commitment satisfactory to everyone.

At meetings there earlier this week it was emphasised that commitment was required by 4 pm Thursday 7 October as the NEB and the Company were meeting on Friday 8 October; without that commitment no submission could be made. A Mini replacement is essential to the marketing strategy of Leyland Cars endorsed by both Government and the Participation system as without such a model for first time buyers our range will be incomplete and other parts of that range endangered, with obvious consequences to the numbers employed in the company. The timing of this project cannot be delayed without considerable increase in investment cost and adverse consequences in the market place.

Mr Whittaker stated that there had to be a significant improvement in performance immediately for any commitment to be credible and acceptable.

The following is an alternative version of the Leyland

Cars bulletin as prepared by Sunday Times journalists (Business News 20 March 1977). It has a Fog Index of 21.

Derek Whittaker has just visited all Plant Participation Committees. He made this point. All employee representatives and all management involved in the new Mini project must promise to improve output as much as is needed. If not, neither he nor his directors will ask the British Leyland Board or the National Enterprise Board to approve any major capital spending plans.

There were full talks about the ADO 88 project by Leyland Cars Joint Management Council – and by the special sub-committee set up by the council to study it. The programme was agreed by both. The council also agreed that the joint management committees and senior representatives in the plants concerned should be shown the programme and asked for their backing. All plants have endorsed the plans except Longbridge. Shopfloor meetings are being held today at Longbridge seeking a deal which will satisfy everyone.

At meetings earlier this week at Longbridge people were told they must promise to give their support by 4 pm Thursday, 7 October. The NEB and the company meet next day (Friday, 8 October). Without this promise no request for money will be made. A new Mini is essential if Leyland is to sell as many cars as it wants. The Government agrees with this. So does everyone in the participation system. Without an up-to-date Mini to attract new first-time buyers, our range will not be complete and other models will be threatened. The effect on jobs is obvious. Delay will increase costs and play into the hand of our rivals.

Mr Whittaker said output had to improve

immediately. If it does not, who will believe any promises made in the future?

The Fog Index: Example 2

Another example of verbal fog (with an index of 138!) is the following, taken from pamphlet LNR(109) which was to be posted up in licensed non-residential establishments, by order of the office of Wages Councils. Read this through carefully until you think you know what it means. Then rewrite it in your own words.

Provided that where the worker normally works for the employer on work to which this Schedule applies for less than 40 hours in a week by reason only of the fact that he does not hold himself out as normally available for work for more than the number of hours he normally works in the week, and the worker has informed his employer in writing that he does not so hold himself out, the guaranteed weekly remuneration shall be the amount payable to the worker at the appropriate hourly rate calculated as in paragraph 1 hereof for the number of hours in the week normally worked by the worker for the employer on work to which this Schedule applies in his usual occupation.

Here is one interpretation of the LNR(109) sentence:
Full time employees covered by the Schedule are entitled to a guaranteed weekly wage. Part time employees are not. A part time employee is one who has informed his employer in writing that he will not normally be available to work as much as forty hours a week. All other employees will count as full time. The guaranteed wage will be based on a forty hour week or on the hours normally worked if more than forty. The appropriate rate for the type of work normally

performed will be applied. The method of calculation is shown in paragraph 1.

After checking with the Department of Employment it turns out that this interpretation, particularly as regards the definition of full and part time workers, it not quite correct. The order LNR(109), which became effective in December 1974, has been superseded by a new order, LNR(139), effective from December 1980. The relevant paragraph in this document reads:

> Where a worker normally works for his employer on work to which this schedule applies for less than 40 hours a week solely because he does not make himself available for work for more than the number of hours he normally works in a week and has so informed his employer in writing, his guaranteed payment shall be the amount to which he would be entitled under paragraphs 3(2) and 4 for working that number of hours.

This has an index of 87 and is a distinct improvement on the earlier version. An attempt has been made to remove the semi-legal style of wording. At the same time it is fair to point out that the orders of the Wages Councils are legally enforceable and the wording must therefore be unambiguous.

Officials are of course aware that there can be a conflict between simplicity of style and unambiguity of meaning. Therefore, in addition to the statutory instruments and other documents which have legal force, advice pamphlets are also prepared. These are written for 'the man in the street'. For example, virtually all drivers who have passed their driving test understand and *do not misinterpret* the Highway Code but do not fully understand (and have probably never even read) the Road Traffic Acts. It is these Acts and not the Highway Code which have the force of law.

There are lessons here for the writer of business and other reports. First, it is better to produce a readable document which the vast majority of people will understand and appreciate than to produce an unreadable and perhaps incomprehensible document which only a specialist will be able to understand. At the same time all reasonable precautions should be taken to avoid ambiguity. Remember that even if your use of words is absolutely correct and no lawyer would misinterpret you, your report is not addressed to a lawyer or to a professor of English. So beware of 'nice points' and 'apparent contradictions' and remember that 'quite' has two quite different meanings.

Self analysis

So far various examples of bad English have been considered: English which is ungrammatical, pompous, long-winded and so on. Now have a look at your own writing and analyse it systematically. Take a page or two at random from a report that you have written. Choose something which is not very recent and not fresh in your mind. This will enable you to consider it objectively. Then:

(1) Read it through. Is the meaning immediately clear? If not, how many times do you have to read it before you are sure you understand it? If the answer is two or more, think what this may mean. Remember that some of the people who are going to look at your report are only going to skim through it once and

then accept it or reject it without giving you a second chance.

(2) Work out the average length of your sentences (number of words) and also note the maximum and minimum sentence lengths. The difference between the longest and the shortest is known as the 'span'. If you think that the existence of one very short sentence or of one very long sentence makes this 'span' a misleading statistic, then perform a more thorough analysis. What proportion of sentences are (a) under ten words, (b) from ten to nineteen words, (c) from twenty to twenty-nine words and (d) thirty words or more? What conclusions do you draw from this?

(3) Count the total number of verbs. Divide these into categories: (a) transitive and active, (b) transitive and passive, (c) intransitive. What is the proportion of verbs in each category? What is the active to passive verb ratio? Bear in mind that intransitive verbs, although weaker than transitive verbs, cannot be passive. There is no hard and fast rule as to what the proportion of active verbs should be but an analysis of the works of a number of well-known authors including Shakespeare and Dickens as well as modern British and American writers indicates that they instinctively use active verbs to speed up the action. On average about one word in eight is an active verb and only one word in twenty-five is an adjective. The style, characterised by the active verb and adjective content varies according to the mood. Indeed it helps to create it. You can create boredom by the use of a flat, monotonous style and the excessive use of vague and weak words. You can create interest by the use of a lively and positive style.

(4) Count the total number of nouns and identify them as either concrete or abstract or, if they do not fit very well into either category, call them 'vague' for lack of a better word. Remember that even a word which is vague on its own can be quite specific in its context or if suitably qualified. For example 'a man' is vague but 'this man' would be referring to a particular man already named. 'A person' is more abstract than 'a man'but less abstract than 'a living creature'. In general you should be as specific as you can since vagueness implies ignorance. If you are ignorant, come out in the open and say that you are not sure, that you can only give an estimate; do not fail to communicate by being vague. Are there any nouns which could have been replaced by verbs? For example, 'The analysis of the data was performed by Mr Smith' could have been written 'The data was analysed by Mr Smith' (passive construction) or 'Mr Smith analysed the data'. This last sentence has only half the number of words which the first sentence has. A single active verb has replaced a noun and a weak passive verb.

(5) Count the number of adjectives and adverbs and express these as percentages of the total number of words in the piece. Consider whether each adjective or adverb was necessary. Strike out those which were superfluous and do the calculation again.

(6) Work out your Fog Index (see page 118). The Index is useful because it takes into account the length of words (number of syllables) as well as the length of sentences (number of words). The implication is that there is some kind of equivalence on the effectiveness scale between a long sentence with short words and a short sentence with long words.

The purpose of this self analysis is not only to improve the style of your English but also to make it more effective. By effective is meant achieving its purpose which is, in the case of reports, to get somebody to do something. The battle is won if and when somebody makes a wise decision on the basis of the information provided in your report. Communication is only half the battle. Now it is a fact that men who have achieved great things are also men who have used language effectively. This language uses (a) a high proportion of active verbs, (b) a high proportion of concrete nouns, (c) relatively few adjectives and adverbs. The sentences vary in length and when they are long they do not ramble; they have rhythm and they pack a punch. Winston Churchill wrote his own speeches and those speeches affected the course of the war. On a lesser plane, reports, letters to the Editor of *The Times*, memoranda to Assistant Secretaries in the Department of Administrative Affairs, advertising jingles, all can be very effective if they are carefully written. If they are badly written they may not be understood, they may be counter-productive, they may never be published. It therefore seems likely that if you can improve your writing you may also improve your chances of success in other spheres. The ability to write good English will not guarantee success any more than being neatly dressed and well groomed when you go for an interview will guarantee that you will get the job. But it helps. If you have something important to say and an opportunity to say it, then, it should be obvious: choose your words carefully. Say it with style. It may make all the difference.

Suggested further reading

Fowler, H. W. and F. G., *Modern English Usage,* OUP, Oxford

Fowler, H. W., *The King's English,* OUP, Oxford
Gowers, Sir Ernest, *The Complete Plain Words,* Penguin Books, Harmondsworth

Mitchell, J., *How to Write Reports,* Collins (Fontana), London

Partridge, E., *Usage and Abusage,* Penguin Books, Harmondsworth, 1963

Perry, Dr. P. J. C. (Editor), *Report Writing,* BACIE
Quiller-Couch, Sir Arthur, *On the Art of Writing,* Guild Books, 1965

Wrenn, C. L., *The English Language,* Methuen, London, 1949